ZENNOVATION

ZENNOVATION

An East-West Approach to Business Success

TOMIO TAKI
ADAM TAKI

CONTRIBUTING EDITOR,
MORTIMER R. FEINBERG, PhD

WILEY

John Wiley & Sons, Inc.

Published by John Wiley & Sons, Inc., Hoboken, New Jersey.
Published simultaneously in Canada.

For general information on our other products and services or for technical support, please
contact our Customer Care Department within the United States at (800) 762-2974,
outside the United States at (317) 572-3993 or fax (317) 572-4002.

Wiley publishes in a variety of print and electronic formats and by print-on-demand.
Some material included with standard print versions of this book may not be included in
e-books or in print-on-demand. If this book refers to media such as a CD or DVD that
is not included in the version you purchased, you may download this material at http://
booksupport.wiley.com. For more information about Wiley products, visit www.wiley.com.

ISBN: 978-1-118-15339-0 (cloth)
ISBN: 978-1-118-22596-7 (ebk)
ISBN: 978-1-118-23928-5 (ebk)
ISBN: 978-1-118-26394-5 (ebk)

Printed in the United States of America
10 9 8 7 6 5 4 3 2 1

Contents

Preface

Former editor-in-chief of *Harper's Bazaar Japan,* Misao Itoh, wrote a book about me called *Manager: Tomio Taki, the Man who Launched Donna Karan.* It was a fantastic text, and I was honored that such a celebrated writer was interested in devoting so much of her own time to telling my story.

After its publication, however, I felt a bit unsettled. The book was great, but it was written in Japanese for a Japanese readership. Although people in Japan may know of my family company, the most extensive international brands that I've founded were launched in the United States. In a way, publishing a book in Japanese for only a Japanese readership excludes Americans and other Anglophones from knowing the history behind the brands and labels I helped create.

A longtime friend and industrial psychologist, Dr. Mortimer Feinberg, insisted I address this concern. Since I am still quite busy, it would have been difficult for me to put pen to paper in a timely manner; therefore, I met with a few capable ghostwriters. The first of these had been a sports journalist, and although he made certain points of my story sound more exciting than I thought they were, he didn't really capture my voice. The second ghostwriter seemed better able to understand how to write a book about entrepreneurship in a straightforward and nondogmatic way. However, I still felt that there was something missing after receiving the draft. Although she understood the concepts founding my train-of-thought and decision-making strategies, the text read a bit on the bare-bones side of a book. The manuscript lacked some cultural nuance and sensitivity.

Although I was not sure what to do, I was interested in hearing what others had to say. I sent the manuscript out to my immediate family to hear their positions. At the time, my son had been a master's student at NYU in the English Department, so I thought he might offer some meaningful insight. I have learned that he tends to be quite critical, which can be immensely helpful despite the difficulties it may present. So after I sent him a draft, I hoped he would read it and give some helpful suggestions so I could go back to the ghost-writer and come to a second draft.

Instead, Adam wound up writing a tome criticizing the original draft. He sent me an e-mail that I started reading; however, there were so many strong positions that I simply gave up. I suppose that's what I get for sending it to someone who has dedicated the lion's share of his master's thesis to etymology and semiotics. He was very opinion-ated and strong-minded, so I returned an e-mail to him asking him to write the draft.

I knew Adam still had a semester or so to finish his master's, so most of the writing had to be done after he'd finished at NYU; however, he began meeting with Mort weekly to go over the broad strokes and devise an outline. Adam had originally suggested revising the current draft and merely adding new anecdotes and supporting evi-dence. Adam completed this task alongside his master's thesis, but he was unhappy with the result. He wanted more focus and direction. I wanted my story to be told but recognized that there were so many fragments that it would be difficult to thread an even, straightforward narrative. Not to say that Don DeLillo's work is less credible because of its fragmentary nature, but it wouldn't make sense for this kind of book in need of a clear beginning, middle, and end.

The summer after completing his coursework, Adam traveled to Japan, South Korea, and Hong Kong to meet with some of my friends and colleagues. He began to parse together my story as he learned about me from other people. For some reason, I have garnered a rep-utation for failing to disclose personal information—partially a result of habit and partially probably the trace of my upbringing steeped in Japanese culture. I differentiate the two because in my younger years,

I was president of my family's 250-year-old textile, fashion, manufacturing, and wholesaling business. As a result, I tended to keep information relatively close to my chest. I think my son learned a lot, as this book covers a lot of information in only so many pages.

After his research, Adam sat down to write my book in English. He chose to focus first on my youth to offer perspective on my upbringing, then on to the most formative and complex experiences of my entrepreneurial career. The book is therefore split into two parts. The first consists mostly of my story heading Takihyo Company Ltd. in Japan through treacherous economic conditions that rival those of the recent financial recession. The second part consists of my entrepreneurial activities in the United States, including building the brands of the Anne Klein Company. I hope you will enjoy reading about some of the problems I faced and the decision-making process I underwent to solve them.

—**Tomio Taki**

Introduction

Over the past 75 years, I have consulted for, financed, or directly managed both private and public companies on nearly every continent. I have been involved in ventures ranging from the birth of high-definition television and video-editing services companies such as the Rebo Group in the United States, to owning and operating private golf clubs in Honolulu, Hawaii, and Raray, France. I helped companies such as Issey Miyake and Wacoal USA rise from the ashes of potential bankruptcy, and I have worked to streamline and grow corporate giants such as Samsung in South Korea and Koor Industries, formerly an arm of the Histadrut, in Israel in the 1980s. I was also responsible for bringing Western fashion to Japanese consumers and was the first to implement mass-manufactured sportswear in the United States when I bought the Anne Klein Company in the early 1970s and launched Anne Klein II, what the fashion industry today calls a bridge line. I am on the board of numerous fashion companies, as well as trustee for a handful of educational institutions in the United States and overseas.

I mention these facts not to gloat, but to delineate the breadth of my life experience. I regret that this book cannot delve into all of these stories and learned lessons. However, I believe that it illustrates whom I have become and what I have learned as an international consultant and manager.

Sharing discourse and advice with businesspersons—ranging from those managing mom-and-pop shops to high-powered executives from across the globe—and therefore exposing myself to the dazzling panoply of cultures and industries has allowed me to transform my perspective. Although I am neither an anthropologist nor a sociologist, I have learned that every nation has a distinct way of conducting business. Language has become less of an obstacle across borders; instead, cultural difference can prompt or hinder communication among businesspersons. Even within many countries, slight differences in latitudinal or longitudinal lines breach social circles. In this light, the only essentialism left in the discussion on offering an international worldview is difference itself.

Alternatively, there are lines of comparison as deep as those of difference. Everyone has goals to accomplish, accompanied by the desire for recognition. Lest we are all forgotten generations from now, we all want to make our mark—not only in the histories of our contemporaries but within native, national narratives. For this very reason, I have chosen to write this book—a testament to my life that my grandchildren and their children can read so that they may learn from my experiences.

With this in mind, I turn to my story as a child who grew up in World War II Japan to become the president of a generations-old textile and fashion company followed by my move to the United States in search of greater opportunity. Much of my personal history has been omitted to fit the scope of this book—not to fragment my story into its various experiences, but to offer a cohesive narrative with all of my most important life lessons. My hope is that every reader may unearth a few points for self-reflection as an entrepreneur, manager, problem solver—or simply an individual.

PART 1

Japan

CHAPTER 1

Optimism, Entrepreneurship, and Raincoats

The Taki family holds a reputation for go-getting. Since I can remember, every Taki who has been president of our family business, Takihyo, has contributed both to the company and to everyday life. My grandfather, Nobushiro Taki, helped transform a once-rural town outside of Nagoya city called Gamagori into a resort town while growing the business. To support his philanthropy, my family and I would go every summer and spring to vacation in Gamagori. My grandfather built hotels and funded shrines and temples; he placed Gamagori on the map as a place for Japanese to rest and relax. Since Takihyo's inception in its humble beginnings, an empire has grown. In short, I had a lot to live up to. I was also the eldest of four boys in a culture of seniority, so it was understood that I would become Takihyo's next leader.

My early childhood was blessed with privilege. I won't hesitate to admit that I was born with a silver spoon in my mouth and could count on my family for everything. I grew up in the industrializing city of Nagoya. At that time, Japan was growing and becoming a part of the modern world that only Europe and America were believed to occupy. However, with that growth of power came avarice; the ideologies underpinning colonial imperialism dominated not only in the West but also in the East. Not unlike Great Britain's colonialization of India and Pakistan, but perhaps most frequently aligned with NSDAP Germany's Blitzkrieg, Japan usurped foreign cities ranging from Nanjing and Shanghai to whole states such as Cambodia, Indonesia, Malaysia, and Vietnam to name a few. The ideological climate placed Japan in a political bind.

I am not a historian, so I will not delve further into historical details, but I think it fair to say that Japan—like so many Euro-American nation-states—took a wrong path. Regardless of Japanese objectives, the end of World War II ushered in a new time—not only for Japan's political development but also for its economic machine. These changes brought with them new realities of everyday life for the nation.

The Second World War changed everything for me. My life of privilege transformed from fond childhood memories into the terror of warfare. At the tender age of 10, I was forced to evacuate my home city of Nagoya-shi, as it had become a target for Allied carpet bombing. Although the area had been predominately agricultural, industry began to build manufacturing plants over the years, including those that were building the so-called meatballs[1] of the Second World War. Concurrent with airplane production came the risk and reality of Allied attack; because of this threat, children from all over the area were evacuated to various camps in the countryside far from the dangers of the war. Although I was terrified to leave, I didn't have a choice. In retrospect, leaving home at such a young age might have been one of the best things that could have happened.

At my camp, I learned to live on my own. I could no longer ask for whatever I wanted. I outgrew many of my childish behaviors there, simply because I worked with other children, cleaning and cooking, as well as tending to the animals and plants we would later consume. Although it took place early in my life, this experience opened my eyes to the world around me. I had never worked as a member of a

---

[1]During the Second World War, Allied troops referred to Japanese fighter planes as "meatballs" because of the large red circles painted on the wings.

team before this. I had only depended on my family for support; I had merely to ask for something, and it would magically appear. The camp put me on an even keel with everyone around me. I learned that my lifestyle had been different from many of the other evacuees. Not everyone had the advantages that I was fortunate to have. Although this view may seem self-evident, it hadn't been for me. The revelation was, to say the least, eye-opening.

I lived with people from varied demographics, including children from Japan's wealthiest and poorest families. This left an indelible signature on my worldview. I saw the distinctions in how people act and react with one another based on the interplay of diverse familial and socioeconomic backgrounds. Not everyone liked the same foods, wore the same clothes, or spoke the same way. Some were more apt to work by themselves, whereas others worked better within a team. Despite how fundamental these differences may seem, watching them in action—and having to cooperate with the others—led me to develop a more nuanced sense of leadership psychology. Learning to appreciate how different people really are, regardless of how narrowly the superficial factors of life may define them, helped me become who I am today.

The most important lesson I learned was that every problem I faced had a solution. This optimism fostered the hope to continue each day knowing that I would again live with my family and be in the comfort of my own home in the near future. I told myself that war and occupation *would* eventually end and that my stay at the camp was temporary. I knew that at some point, there would be peace again in Japan.

I learned the value of this optimism in the darkest of times. Besides, sitting around feeling sorry for myself was not an option: if I were to get bogged down wallowing in despair and fail to cook enough dinner, neither I nor some of the other evacuees would eat that night. The severity of the situation forced me to develop a sense of self-reliance that stayed with me for the rest of my life—thereby allowing reason and principles to guide me. As you will read later, I—like most people—have been dealt a number of unfortunate cards. However, the diligence and patience I cultivated in my early years prompted me to work through what I believe were the toughest challenges. Keeping an optimistic view of the future has enabled me to enjoy many successes—in both my corporate and personal life.

The war had ended by the time I was in fifth grade, and so I returned home. I matriculated into Taki Gakuen,[2] an elementary-through-college preparatory school that my grandfather had established but which, by that time, my father was managing. I had been reunited with my family for the first time in years; however, my stay there was not long. Neither my father nor I felt comfortable with my being a student at the school; we worried that others would think that I would be favored. My father also believed my enrollment might incite unethical behavior among the faculty—who might be inclined to give me better grades for less work because my father was the principal—or bullying from my peers. After a couple semesters, I transferred to Tokai Gakuen in the center of Nagoya.

Although the distance between my family's house and Nagoya was only about 7 miles, the train ride was terrifying for a little boy. The cars were cramped and uncomfortable, and mounting and dismounting was quite dangerous; it was a challenge for adults to get on and off the train without injuring themselves, so you might imagine the difficulty faced by a young child. After I discussed with my parents the concern that I could get hurt on these train rides, they decided to board me near the Tokai School. Although I did not live with my family anymore, the commute to school became much easier—and I was no longer worried about the crowded trains. I stayed in this boarding house until my sophomore year of high school when my father decided to relocate the family into the center of Nagoya city.

I rarely got to spend time with my family, except for short holiday vacations. Unfortunately, I could not live with them, and I was about to enter Keio University. My family's influence over me had therefore been somewhat absent. I spent the majority of the most formative childhood years learning to become independent and self-reliant at the evacuee camp and at boarding houses. Further complicating my family life was the fact that my father had always been very busy running Takihyo and our family's school. As a result, I did not have the opportunity to learn much from him other than an understanding of his work ethic.

---

[2] *Gakuen* means "junior high" in Japanese.

Although I had gone through the rigors of learning to become self-reliant at a young age, the kinds of problems that most adults face had yet to confront me. At Keio, I began learning about life through metaphor, academics, and my social life. I joined the university's basketball team, which was a year-round extracurricular activity. I wound up completing most of my exams on the road or between practices. I spent much less time in class because of this commitment, which forced me to learn how to structure my time. We practiced nearly every day, and we traveled all around Japan to compete. The stress of excelling both in my classes and on the court taught me more about myself and how to become more responsible than ever before. Yet I cannot take total credit for this process; I had the opportunity to be mentored by a brilliant team leader.

One of the most influential people in my life was my basketball coach, Mr. Taketomi. Not only was he a good coach, but he also had a mastery of leadership psychology. His three points about playing basketball are ingrained in my memory, and I've found it to be immensely fruitful to apply his leadership psychology to problem solving. His three points are as follows: first, when playing basketball—or any sport—you must bend your knees before you jump. If you don't, the height of the jump is greatly compromised. Because knee-bending allows the leg muscles to work in unison with the rest of the body, you can use this combined momentum and strength to catapult the body upward. This first tenet led me to understand a much more overarching principle: in more practical terms, knee-bending equates with logistical preparation. I learned that if I wanted to do something, I would have to make sure to bend my knees, to be prepared, to handle any foreseeable problems posed by various circumstances.

Second, Taketomi proposed that winning is impossible if you don't know the competition. This tenet covers more psychological ground than does knee-bending, but it is a part of the overall preparation in setting and accomplishing a goal. Learning about the opponent—whether it's in basketball or in a business venture—is a part of any winning strategy. And the better your understanding of what you're up against, the better your strategic results. In basketball, for example, knowing the opponent's offensive plays sheds light on how to prepare better defensive tactics. A good defense has more steals, rebounds, and blocks—all of which result in the other team scoring fewer points, which in turn increases the chances of victory. Understanding one's opponent—whatever the situation—offers a psychological advantage over the competition.

The last but perhaps most important lesson I learned: without a loser, there is no winner. Losing always has a negative psychological impact in any sport or scenario. After training for so many hours, doing countless drills, and practicing painstaking strategic counter measures, raw skill and psychological toughness always seem to divide the winners from the losers. However, there are upsets in the real world. The beauty in Taketomi's theory is its inherent optimism. Even great teams lose. Hard work and dedication lead to victory, even if a victory reads as an "L" on the standings; staying optimistic and prepared yield the most promising results.

I found that I could apply these three points to almost any real-world situation by asking one simple question: What do I want to accomplish? A goal-oriented approach to problem solving has always offered me good results. Although there are countless ways to solve a problem, each task has only one goal. Throughout this book, I will reference the times I asked this question again and again, in every business venture. Although I cannot guarantee managerial success to every reader, I hope that my methods shed light on an alternative approach to problem solving.

Before I discuss my early work experience, I'd like to touch briefly on my first taste of international management and recruiting as Keio University's basketball team manager. Despite how young I was at the time, I was—and still am—eager to learn from others, regardless of who they are or what they represent. As a young Japanese man with an aim to make my basketball team the best, I looked for alternative leadership. Taketomi had been a great group leader, but basketball was relatively new to Japan—and I was looking for guidance from someone who had extensive experience playing in more competitive circles.

I read in the newspapers about a man named Leonard Craven. He had formerly been a basketball player for UCLA in the States. Well aware of UCLA's Division One standing and reputation, I started talking with Taketomi and a couple of our other coaches. I asked if it would be possible to hire Craven to help us with drills and plays, as I was sure his experience could become a great asset. At the time, Craven had been stationed at Haneda Air Force Base, not far from Tokyo, so I went to Haneda in hopes of meeting with him.

I knocked on Craven's door, and we sat down and began discussing the possibilities of him coming to Keio to help train my team. Craven was incredibly excited about the idea, but he was unsure if it would hinder his capacities to fulfill his military duties. By the end of the conversation, Craven committed to asking his superior, who at the time was a two-star general in the Air Force.

Craven's commanding officer was incredibly excited at the prospect, and his opportunism worked in my favor. The general jumped at the idea of Craven helping to coach us; perhaps he hoped he'd receive a third star for working to make agreements of international cooperation on levels beyond the political. The following week, I returned to Craven's office to find a sign on his door: "Leonard Craven: Keio University Basketball Coach." I was surprised how well the whole situation worked itself out. Craven then became one of our head coaches until leaving his station at Haneda to return to the United States.

Despite this experience, however, I was hardly capable of running a business on my own at the age of 22. I needed more than what Taketomi taught me; although I had learned a lot from the game, playing basketball did not equip me to become a responsible adult. After graduating from college, my father asked my step-uncle, Chubei Ito, if I could have an apprenticeship at his company, Osaka-based Itochu. Although Itochu began as a yarn distribution company with strong familial ties to my father and thus Takihyo, Itochu eventually grew to become one of Japan's largest conglomerates. It included divisions that ranged from textiles to aerospace and nuclear energy. Whether it was my step-uncle's love or trust that got me there, I will never fathom; but I was (un)fortunate enough to assume many responsibilities immediately. One of my superiors had passed away and the other was transferred to another position within Itochu. My new superior expected me to accomplish the work of these two former employees along with handling my assigned position. Without much of a choice, I undertook these three positions simultaneously until we could hire new employees. My boss offered me a crash course in the business with long hours and heavy emotional strain. This was my first glimpse of the corporate structure.

However painful, this experience elucidated an integrated, more comprehensive take on problem solving. I learned that if the finances of a business needed work, the marketing sector could lend a hand. I also quickly figured out that different positions—although varied in their immediate goals and perspectives—were tightly woven in the overarching corporate structure. Most businesses appear to have separate divisions and purposes for different titles. In the end, however, if a company is failing, those different divisions and departments are likely not working together. Through my experience of having to shoulder the responsibility of three distinct positions consolidated into one, I observed firsthand the interconnectivity of corporate structure.

Around the same time, I met my first wife. Yoko and I were married the second year of my stay at Itochu. By the third year, we were blessed with twin boys. Although I loved my twins from the bottom of my heart, the timing made the last year at Itochu very difficult. I went to work early in the morning to return home and take care of the children with Yoko. In the first year after birth, the children slept a lot and had irregular feeding times—one at midnight and another at three in the morning. Sometimes one would get hungry at two in the morning and the other at three. Their cries woke Yoko and me; then one of us would feed one if not both of them. I loved them, but having twins was a much larger responsibility than I had previously imagined. I was in a state of constant physical fatigue. I hardly slept that last year at Itochu. Luckily for me, my father wanted me to return to Nagoya; after spending so much time away from home, I was happy about the change.

I left my apprenticeship at Itochu not only with knowledge of how the different arms of the corporate body fit together, but with two healthy children and a caring wife. This was a great time in my life; I had learned a lot about certain facets of how a successful business operates. Although I found this experience fruitful, my father was not ready to give me much responsibility upon my return. He wanted to test my newly found skills and show me how a business can work from the ground up.

For the first month, I worked in shipping and receiving. I packed and opened boxes. Although I was not in a position with a lot of responsibility, my father believed that it was necessary for me to understand more than just how different parts of the corporate structure functioned; he wanted me to learn the day-to-day logistics firsthand. After that first month, he put me in charge of the import-export division. I primarily worked in warehouses, managing inventories and distributing incoming and outgoing products.

During the Second World War and the following occupation, Takihyo had to undergo a number of changes. The government had full control of industry, manufacturing, and distribution. Politicians decided that the nation should receive rations of food, clothing, you-name-it during wartime. As a result, Takihyo temporarily stopped wholesaling clothing. By the end of the war and the beginning of the occupation, those who survived returned to work for Takihyo but had little to do. The company then branched out to accommodate the employees by starting a nonclothing business—selling household goods like pots, pans, buckets, mops, brooms, and anything else that one could find at a local hardware store.

Near the end of the occupation, however, things settled back to normal at Takihyo. In 1953, the organization returned to wholesaling traditional Japanese kimonos and futon fabrics. We did not close down the other established divisions, but the wholesaling of textiles again became a main focus. When I started working at Takihyo's import-export division in 1959, I was responsible for all different kinds of inventory. However, my father could tell that I was not challenged by this post. He saw promise in what I had achieved at Itochu and he believed I could handle more responsibility.

My father went on a trip to Okinawa arranged by the Okinawan Chamber of Commerce. While there, my father committed to starting a joint venture with a landowner and a large department store chain called Yamagataya in Okinawa. The landowner would supply the property on which a factory could be built to manufacture clothing; the department store would help fund half of the venture, and Takihyo would fund the other half and manage it. After all the years of wholesaling Japanese textiles and kimonos, my father wanted to open a new operation in Okinawa to manufacture clothing made from our textiles division.

After I had been working for three months at Takihyo, my father asked me to go to Okinawa. I was taken aback, to say the least. "Why do you want me to go to Okinawa?" I wanted to know. He told me that it was because we were building a joint-venture company.

I then asked what kind, and the answer came back: "a sewing factory." Although we at first went back and forth a bit like the game Twenty Questions, my father ultimately left me in charge of the venture with no strings attached. I asked what he wanted to manufacture in the sewing factory and he replied, "I don't know. Don't ask any more questions because I don't have any more answers." As such, Father made it *my* job to figure out what to manufacture and where to sell it. With little knowledge of the textile business, I had to bend my knees a bit before making the jump.

The first move I made was to go to Okinawa. Some background on the political situation in 1959: America took control of the prefecture after winning the Battle of Okinawa in 1945. Until the Treaty of Mutual Cooperation and Security of 1972, Okinawa was considered American soil and was heavily populated by US Air Force bases. The United States signed Okinawa over to the Japanese with the 1972 agreement, but until 1975, the Ryukyu Islands (of which Okinawa was the largest) had been a home for many American Marines and members of the US Air Force. For that reason, I thought establishing a factory in Okinawa was geared toward international rather than domestic interests.

Since the beginnings of modern international trade, the United States has attempted to protect American business by setting up quota systems. There are countless restrictions on almost all goods coming into the United States. However, because pre-1972 Okinawa had been considered part of the United States, there was no quota— and the number of Okinawan garments that could enter the United States was unlimited. Although Takihyo was and is based in Japan, my father figured we could circumvent any governmental restrictions on importing Okinawan goods to the continental United States because the goods manufactured in this sewing factory were technically on US soil. At the time, the most stringent quota restrictions for a non-US business had been on cotton-based goods. However, the problem was further complicated and I needed to take a step back.

I asked myself, "What do I want to accomplish?" If I were to build a sewing factory to make any kind of clothing, what would be most lucrative? It had been rumored that the United States would return Okinawa back to the Japanese government; however, reintroducing Okinawa into Japan would have its consequences.

The standardization of the Japanese government over economic affairs would play a role in how a business could be run in Okinawa—the salaries of our employees would spike. Because the Ryukyu Islands had never been fully incorporated into everyday Japanese life before the war, the pay scales in Okinawa were much lower than in mainland Japan. The answer to my question yielded yet another question. After some deliberation, I figured out my plan.

I wanted to establish a branch of Takihyo that could bear the political winds of the time. If I decided to manufacture a particular product, I wanted labor costs to be minimal so that the factory's overhead could compensate for any changes in the Okinawan pay scales. If and when Okinawa became a part of Japan again, I also wanted the product's profits to compensate for changes in the Okinawan quota system. This would allow me to build a factory that could theoretically meet both long- and short-term goals.

Once I established these goals, it was much easier to come up with an idea for what to manufacture in the new factory. To overcome any future rise in manufacturing costs, the factory would have to produce something that had a low manufacturing cost and a higher gross margin. As I mentioned earlier, a number of people were involved in this venture, and they too were a part of this discourse. When I arrived at Okinawa, the factory was about 85 percent completed. The remaining 15 percent was our time to plan logistics and discuss what type of product we would manufacture. A lot of brainstorming occurred in that limited amount of time—so much so that a number of conflicts rose among us. On the second to last day of my visit, I told our partners, "Tomorrow we must decide on something to produce that meets our criteria." We would sleep on it and come to a decision the next morning.

The following morning I approached the rest of the investors with a somewhat atypical suggestion. I didn't propose that we make blouses or dresses made of cotton; instead I suggested making raincoats. Although in terms of its chemical makeup cotton is not the best fabric with which to make raincoats, it is the most commonly used. Raincoats also provided an easy answer to a complex question. Despite using little more material than dresses, raincoats appear far more valuable to consumers. People will pay much more for a coat than a dress—because the profit margins for the coats are that much higher, I thought this venture could be self-sustainable despite Okinawa's inevitable return to Japan.

The partners asked me if I knew how to make raincoats. Of course, I had little experience and no idea. My father did not know either. He had been a part of the traditional Japanese garment industry, far from Western markets. I figured that I could use the rest of the time I had until the factory's completion to get these logistics in order. I had previously met Christopher Cheng from Hong Kong's Win Tie company through my father's close relationship with Chris's father. He was the first person who came to mind whom I could ask how to manufacture raincoats. Cheng was making denim jeans, so I assumed that he probably knew how to make raincoats out of similar materials. I also had heard that Cheng too had been interested in making raincoats for sale in the United States.

However, I was in for a letdown, because Chris had no idea; in fact, he had hoped that his father might have the answer. But because Win Tie had only made denim jeans since its inception, Chris's father didn't know how to make cotton raincoats either. However, he did make an interesting suggestion. He told us to go find a tailor from Shanghai in Hong Kong—because a good Shanghai tailor can make any garment! So Chris and I searched Hong Kong to find a couple of tailors who knew raincoats well. Chris took one to set up a sewing factory in Hong Kong, and I sent the other to work for us in Okinawa. Because the factory had yet to be completed, I wanted someone who knew how to make the raincoats for the sewing factory in a way that would maximize productivity and efficiency. I knew I wasn't in any position to organize how the plant should sew, and the person who did know should spearhead the sewing process.

I also needed to find a buyer. Because Takihyo had wholesaled only Japanese traditional garments, neither I nor my father had any idea where I could look to sell the raincoats. Takihyo had laid no tracks for my venture on American soil. I got on a flight to New York to try to figure everything out. On my first day there, I went to a large department store (I believe it was Macy's). I walked into the raincoat section and asked the salesperson where she happened to buy the raincoats in the store, because I thought she might know the supplier. She told me there was a buyer who had another office on another floor. So I went to the buyer's office, and after a brief conversation she kicked me out. She asked me how long I had been in the raincoat business and if I had a sample. Since I had neither experience nor a sample, I was of no use to her.

The following day I returned to the buyer's office to ask her some more questions. For fear of bothering her too much, I kept it short: "Who do you buy your raincoats from?" She pointed me to a particular export company that had an office in New York. I went to visit the office and received the same questions as I had from the buyer at Macy's. I neither wanted to waste their time nor my own, so I left. Although my time in New York was a bit frustrating, I learned something new: how to bend my knees in a new environment trying to sell new products. In short, I learned that I needed to have a sample or a relationship to get things off the ground.

That same day, I went to the Japanese consulate in New York to get some advice. Because the Japanese government had been taking strides to develop economic relationships with the United States, I thought there might be someone to help me there—but no such luck. I spent the last day of my trip visiting an organization called Jetro USA. Known for its networking functions and business development support, I thought this organization would be my best bet. Unfortunately, I didn't get any help there, either.

After a long and hard day, I returned to my hotel room. I sat on the bed and stared at the wall while I tried to come up with a solution. Without any experience or history manufacturing raincoats, selling Takihyo-made raincoats was becoming a daunting task. Neither the government nor an organization geared toward business development could help me develop a sound strategy or business contacts. What made matters worse was that despite the fact that Takihyo was a well-known company in Japan, the name meant very little to an American working in the fashion industry. At this point, the only thing I could do was try to remain optimistic.

All of a sudden, after much tautological brainstorming, Chris Cheng called me on the phone. He urged me to come to Hong Kong to meet a man named Roger Spiegel. Spiegel had been the raincoat buyer for Best & Co., a department store that had recently declared bankruptcy and closed down. However, Spiegel wanted to continue his work buying raincoats for distribution in the United States.

Finally I had found the break I'd needed. Spiegel traveled to Hong Kong in search of a raincoat supplier in the Far East to jump-start his new wholesaling company. Since there was no competition in Hong Kong—and since Spiegel had also been starting his company from scratch—he was eager to come aboard to help with my raincoats as well as Chris Cheng's project to offer American consumers two different raincoats of high quality at incredibly low prices.

First, however, we needed to find a raincoat to emulate for production in Okinawa. We had no grand plans to introduce new innovations in raincoat design. Instead, we wanted to manufacture a product that looked and felt similar to expensive ones but that sold at a third of the price. Spiegel knew the fads and the staples of the business, so I asked him to bring me three different cotton raincoat samples. We chose one, and then had the tailor tear them at the seams to make fresh patterns. The patterns would guide us through the difficult part of putting the raincoats together; this would allow us to make the raincoats without coming up with a design from scratch. We could copy someone else's design, charge much less for labor, and sell the product at a more competitive price.

After its production, Spiegel labeled the raincoat Briarcliff. I think Spiegel chose this Western-sounding name because he thought it would add some credibility to the brand. He may have wanted consumers to associate the raincoat's name with Briarcliff Manor in upstate New York.

Of course, the design was not entirely copied; we did make certain modifications. We found that shortening the coat as little as an inch or two on the back could eventually yield enough fabric for another raincoat's outer shell. Because we were using less fabric, we lowered production costs and augmented profit potential. The search for new ways to meet competitive prices became something of a game rather than a challenge—and this kind of thinking allowed for creative ways to bring in more profit.

Unfortunately, once the United States returned Okinawa to the Japanese government, pay scales changed to become much higher than we had estimated when establishing the sewing factory. We had no idea that Japan would grow as quickly as it did, and we did not expect per capita incomes to rise so high. As a result of these changes, we had to close the factory and end the production of Briarcliff raincoats. However, while it was up and running—and Okinawa had been under American rule—this venture grew to become very profitable. I was pleased with the results, and so was my father. I was ecstatic that everything had worked out despite the odds against me.

My career as an international entrepreneur began with this raincoat venture. I was fortunate that my father had put me in this position where I had to search for solutions to tough problems. Tackling these issues required me to develop a certain sense of managerial creativity; however, I give my sense of optimism credit for most of this accomplishment. This venture had been the most terrifying for me because there were times when I had no idea what to do. However, step by step, I came to a conclusion. With determination, good luck, and forward-thinking, I was able to make the venture a success. My basketball coach's teachings came in handy, too, as I was maneuvering my way through this new environment. I saw where I needed to put more of my energy in the future—how I could bend my knees a bit more. I developed a more complete understanding of how different methods of manufacturing a product could yield higher profit margins and saw firsthand how a little more preparation could yield dramatic positive gains. I have tried to carry these lessons with me throughout my career.

Optimism Is Intelligent

My father cautioned me, "You may be a peacock one day and a feather duster the next." In other words, we will all experience misfortune and failure at one point or another. However, we must remain optimistic rather than cynical as we contemplate the possible certainty of events going downhill.

Psychologists used to believe that cynics were somehow smarter than optimists. As the saying goes, "Optimists believe in the best of all possible worlds and pessimists worry that they may be right." For a long time, optimism was considered the

(continued)

(continued)

hallmark of stupidity. Early psychologists believed that optimists were somehow naive, and that skeptics were somehow smarter. However, we've come to find that this is not the case—not even close.

A new paradigm called the Psychology of Optimism has emerged. The theory was first formulated by Professor Martin Seligman at the University of Pennsylvania, who found that well-rounded optimists are healthier, live longer, and are better able to cope with life challenges. Optimists, quite simply, live more fulfilled lives than pessimists. They are more equipped to relish the possibility of succeeding in the future; therefore, they can tackle today's problems with more confident expectations. The prospect of failure does not paralyze optimists' actions, whereas some pessimists opt to reject before *being* rejected because they fear failure. "I didn't really try" appears to excuse negative thinkers. These excuses, however, will only ensure that a person never succeeds. Optimists give their full effort and more.

One has to risk the possibility of failure to succeed. In the depths of the Great Depression, President Franklin Roosevelt's optimism lifted the spirit of the nation, giving Americans new hopes and dreams. After Roosevelt delivered his famous "The only thing we have to fear is fear itself" speech, I remember my father expressing his relief; he felt confident that the country was in good hands.

Optimists like Roosevelt are not starry-eyed space cadets. They don't believe "everything will come up roses." They recognize that harsh realities accompany worthy achievements. During the darkest days of World War II, Winston Churchill put up a poster in the war room that read: "There is no room for pessimism." When you have a mental choice you must—as the ditty goes, and as Tomio Taki believes—"Move your feet to the sunny side of the street."

The American Psychologist recently reanalyzed the mortality data for a group of children first studied by psychologist Lewis Terman in 1922. The research found that on average the most cheerful children died earlier, and that earlier deaths might have been partially caused by a more careless attitude toward health. They were somewhat more likely to drink, smoke, and take other risks to their health.

Furthermore, particularly conscientious children lived longer, healthier lives on average. This makes sense, the article said, because "a conscientious person will probably head to the doctor at the first sign of trouble, avoiding later, more serious problems." The article continues: "People tried to generalize and say a trait like cheerfulness or neuroticism is good or bad, but, sometimes it's good to worry, and sometimes it's not—it depends on the situation." Thus, the researchers found that it's not so much the trait that's important, but knowing when to apply it to a particular situation. Perhaps the important thing is to remember to balance optimism with a grounded sense of reality. This thinking, however, is much older than modern thought. As Milton wrote in *Paradise Lost*, "The mind is its own place, and in it self can make a Heav'n of Hell, a Hell of Heav'n."

Mortimer R. Feinberg, PhD

CHAPTER 2

Losing My Father

In 1959, I applied to Harvard Business School and was accepted to begin in the fall semester of 1960. It was unusual for a Japanese businessman to attend an American university, but I was eager to gain a fresh perspective on business from an entirely different culture. Although Japan underwent some changes, the nation's corporate culture had remained relatively unchanged since the beginning of World War II. My limited exposure to life and culture outside of Japan made me feel isolated—and I feared this isolation would stunt my growth as an entrepreneur. I wanted to see and experience more of the world.

I also hoped that going to the United States would help me to master the English language. Without a doubt, learning to speak English fluently could yield only positive results. My experience hiring Leonard Craven when I was at Keio provided an excellent opportunity for me to work on my English; however, it had been a few years since that time, and I needed more practice. Moving to the United States would also give me a more nuanced perspective of how people act and react and how other people maintain a cultural identity different from what I knew. The diversity of American demographics appeared to offer something that the racially homogeneous Japan did not. I knew that living and studying in America would change how I thought—and would help me become a full-fledged member of the international community.

These views about the importance of diversity and internationalism, however, were not common in Japan. Although steeped in my culture, I have always felt a bit different. Others have noted that I never acted or treated others as a Japanese, but as someone with a different understanding of the world. The stereotypes surrounding Japanese businesspersons hold an inkling of truth. The 500 years of near-complete isolation previous to modernization may have fostered the misinformed mores of modern Japanese society. In addition, the Japanese language lends itself to this kind of thinking, since the Japanese are the only people speaking it—and thus the only people who can communicate to one another effectively. This language, based on social and cultural cues unlike any other, can make the layers of Japanese culture and society appear unclear and ambiguous to outsiders. I recognized this early in my studies and found that in order to bridge cultures and communicate successfully, I would have to abandon those social cues and replace them with a more complex approach; only then would I find a place in the international arena.

However, as it turned out, I would not be able to attend Harvard University or travel to the United States on an extended basis. My father died just as I was notified of my acceptance to business school. Until this day, I am not sure exactly what happened. One night he returned home laughing, smiling, and singing from spending time with friends at a nearby lounge. He was joyful and at the end of the evening he said good night to everyone, then retired to bed.

At the time, my youngest brother, Shigeo, was only 10 and afraid of the dark, so he would sleep with my father frequently when he was too scared to sleep alone. In the middle of the night, my father began trembling and woke Shigeo. Shigeo asked him what he was doing, then turned on a light on the bedside table. As my brother has recounted, my father's face was changing colors and it appeared as if he were choking. Shigeo screamed for help. My mother called a doctor, but by the time he arrived at the house, it was too late. There was nothing that could be done to rescue my father. He was only 52, and there were no warning signs of illness.

The loss of my father was devastating to me, but for some of my brothers it was much worse. Unlike my brothers, I had lived away from my father for the majority of my life. When I did live with him, my father had always been busy running the family company and school. This is not to say that we never spent time together; however, most of our adult interactions were business related. My brothers, on the other hand, spent much more quality time with my father and thus had developed much stronger personal relationships with him. Their youth magnified this tragedy as well.

In the United States, gender no longer determines who the family's breadwinner will be, and in this respect, American culture remains fairly straightforward. In Japan, on the other hand, there are layers of unspoken tradition. A hierarchy based upon seniority often overlaps with a paternalism within the family. I therefore became responsible for my younger siblings' and mother's well-being. Although I was too young to handle such enormous responsibility, I had to accept it. I also wanted to prove myself not only as a capable businessman but also as a good son and brother. So, at the age of 26, I was forced to become the head of my family.

I could not anticipate my father's death when applying to Harvard. He was young, and I had been looking forward to spending more time with him to make up for the time we had lost due to the war and other personal factors. I wanted the opportunity to learn from him, as he had learned from his father. I wanted to be closer with him and gain some of the wisdom he had garnered during all the years as Takihyo's president and father of a family of four. I looked forward to a gradual and deliberate introduction into the family business and to life.

I deeply mourned my father's death, but I also had to be a strong figure within the household. I had to show my strength in the face of trauma. What made matters worse was the fact that because my father had been so young, he had made no estate plan. There was no writ to consult when distributing his wealth. Therefore, I was forced to inherit his positions in the Takihyo company as well as his assets. In terms of my family, my brothers were too young to know what to do with their shares, and my mother gave me her own to oversee. I held total fiduciary responsibility for my family.

Although many may dream to inherit, it became a curse rather than a blessing for me. The lack of planning for my father's inheritance caused us to travel the default route when paying inheritance taxes, which in Japan were, and still are, astronomical. Moreover, because most of my father's wealth had been invested in the Takihyo company—and it had been a family company for a couple hundred years—selling the shares was not an option. Liquidating large portions of the company to pay taxes would compromise the family business. If I were to have taken that route, the Taki family would no longer own the majority of Takihyo; instead, the company would be in the hands of the buyers. I knew that we could not sell those shares for fear of losing the company that had been passed down from father to son for many generations. When my father was alive, he had opened a wide path for me to do and accomplish whatever I wanted. I appreciated his willingness to let me grow and learn about new ventures. I wanted to ensure that I would be able to give my brothers the same experience, so I had to forfeit my plans to attend Harvard and take on these new responsibilities as head of my family and of Takihyo.

A close family friend of ours who happened to run what was then Tokai Bank (but is now a part of Tokyo–Mitsubishi UFJ Bank) asked how things were going for me and for the family. I had to be honest with him. A part of me wanted to find a way to make it without help from others, but I knew that this simply wasn't possible. I therefore asked for a loan during our conversation. At the time, I had neither the income nor the savings to pay the inheritance taxes for my family. I needed money and I needed to budget our family's spending. I also knew that I would have been rejected if I had gone anywhere else for the loan. I was very fortunate to have this man as a friend; otherwise, I don't know what would have happened to us or the family business. I was young and with little experience of the business world. My salary could not support a family of six. How could I have repaid such a substantial loan with so little to offer? I struck a deal with my friend to repay over the course of 10 years—even though I wasn't quite sure at the time how I was going to do so.

For those 10 years, I began making enough money to support my family; however, I also had to pay to put my brothers through college. I was young and motivated, but the circumstances were trying. I had a demanding personal life; I had twin babies and had to take care of my younger brothers and mother along with the family business. I was forced to fill my father's shoes at both Takihyo and Taki Gakuen, the family school, among other ventures.

Emotional Maturity

Few are certain they know what a mature person looks like—
his makeup, the way he meets the challenge of his job and his
family responsibilities, his outlook on the world. Psychologists
and psychiatrists are all agreed on this: the clue to personal success is the growth, or the progressive achievement, of emotional
maturity.

That stage of development which we generally refer to as
maturity implies that an individual has the ability to respond to a
variety of stimuli without resorting to fight or flight. A mature
person is able to deal with problems objectively. His interests
are broader and deeper than mere survival. He is able to operate
with a degree of independence and a firm sense of reality.

Obviously, then, maturity is a tremendous asset. In fact, on
or off the job, the word *maturity* has become a glittering seal of
approval—a stamp of having what it takes. The following are 10
characteristics that can help you recognize maturity in yourself
and others:

1. Self-acceptance
2. Respect of others
3. Acceptance of responsibility
4. Confidence
5. Openness to experience and patience
6. A sense of humor
7. Resilience to pick yourself up after trauma
8. Capacity to make decisions under pressure
9. Effective management of aberrations
10. A strong set of guiding principles

I believe without a doubt that Tomio Taki has all of these traits.
He dealt with his father's death in an incredibly mature way.

(continued)

(continued)

There were many problems confronting him simultaneously, and he confronted each one with a cool hand—without batting an eye. Tomio's behavior in this incident reminds me of Winston Churchill's comment in the darkest days of the Second World War.

Mortimer R. Feinberg, PhD

CHAPTER 3

Changing Takihyo with American Brashness

Ten months after I joined Takihyo and established the raincoat factory in Okinawa, my father passed away. I suggested to the company's executives that my mother take my father's place as Takihyo's president and that I take the office of vice president. I felt that as a carrier of the Taki name with an older, more experienced face, my mother would create a better image for the company. I must admit that I was terrified to replace my father at the company so suddenly. I feared the responsibility, and I worried that I might not live up to the successes that people had come to expect from my lineage. Having my mother as the figurehead would allow me to avoid bearing sole responsibility.

At only 26, I did not believe I was ready for such intense responsibility. The executives, however, vetoed my suggestion. Perhaps they weren't ready for a woman to run a company so anchored in tradition; perhaps Japan's culturally deep-seated paternalism made me president. Although I had disagreed and fought with these same men before, I knew I wouldn't win the battle this time. It not only had been a tradition within the Taki family to pass the torch from father to son, but, despite my lack of managerial experience, I was technically of age. The board believed in me and what I could offer the company—perhaps more than I believed in myself. With the board's trust and my own motivation, I could only do my best and embrace my new role as president.

I therefore was forced to rescind my acceptance to Harvard University's B-school and take over Takihyo. Having worked only in the import-export division, I had little knowledge of the company—and even less knowledge of the kimono business itself. I had never made a kimono, and everyone else in the company had been in the business for many years.

Thus, I had to ask a lot of questions to get the information I needed. There was no learning curve in the business and there were others waiting to test my knowledge and legitimacy as Takihyo's president. To say that I was not comfortable in my new position would be an understatement. I had only my past experiences to provide a foundation for my future endeavors. I reminisced over my basketball coach's words: prepare yourself, know your opposition, be aware of your surroundings. But how could I run a company whose products I did not know?

At the time, Japan was transforming, well on its way to becoming a pacifist, democratic nation-state. There was no defense force, and the government money that once had paid for the military was redirected to rebuild and improve the country. I felt change happening all around me, and as the new president of a company older than America itself, I knew that Takihyo needed to adapt. These feelings, however, were just that; they were emotions, not evidence. Before I would make a drastic move on behalf of the company, I would need hard facts to support my gut feelings.

As the new president, I wanted to learn about the company by starting at the bottom and working my way up. I had to see how the company made its money and how it had been sustaining itself all those years. As part of my learning experience, I asked for all of the invoices and payables to be sent to me after any purchase or sale had been made. I wanted to know how much people were spending and how much Takihyo would make on each sale. Each day, I went through stacks upon stacks of invoices—not only to learn about the company, but also to question the decisions that the other executives made. I would ask, for example, why certain fabrics were bought at certain prices and if there were anywhere else we could purchase those fabrics at a better price. I would also ask questions about the manufacturing process, and why it cost more to handle some fabrics than others. This research was painstaking, but the results were clear to me. I now had the facts to move forward with my strategic plans for Takihyo.

I saw the traditional garment and fabric business in Japan moving on a downward slope. As a young man, I—and my peers—rarely wore the traditional garb. As such, the kimono had shifted from an everyday necessity to a specialized market. In addition, many of the fabrics needed to produce the traditional kimonos were growing increasingly expensive and Takihyo's profits in the kimono market were negligible. Underwear, for instance, could be sold at a high volume with little profit; however, it still provided the manufacturers and wholesalers a decent margin of income. Kimonos, on the other hand, did not sell in such quantities. I knew that if a declining business were at the heart of Takihyo, I would not be able to sustain the business into the future. The evidence of this was indisputable; yet it wasn't until I finished my research on my family's company that it became entirely apparent.

By the time I became head of the company, most men were no longer wearing kimonos, no matter what the occasion. That trend was sure to seep into the female way of life in Japan's future. Although elegant and beautiful, kimonos are cumbersome; they're best suited for ceremonial activities, not daily ones. I knew deep down that the future of the clothing business was in the West. A few other Japanese clothing companies had begun to dabble in the Western clothing business with some success. However, their efforts were not full force. In a typically Japanese fashion, companies tend to make changes gradually—which often also means that it takes a long time to accomplish anything significant. I reasoned that Takihyo would have to make a similar move into Western clothing; however, instead of taking baby steps like our competitors, I felt that our company should thrust itself into the new, emerging business of women's fashion.

I expressed my thoughts to the other executives at Takihyo, and the consensus was strongly against me. They essentially argued, "If it ain't broke, don't fix it." After all, they reasoned, Takihyo had managed to run a successful business for the last 200 years—and we were already generating more than $30 million in revenues during the first year of my presidency. What was the point of changing? Yet unlike my fellow leaders, I feared the stagnation of the company. The way I saw it, a stagnant company could be compared to stagnant water: if you let water sit for too long, bacteria grows, and the water becomes undrinkable.

One morning, I announced to the company that we could not remain in the kimono business and that Takihyo would have to retool. To that end, as of April 1, 1963, Takihyo no longer distributed or manufactured any traditional Japanese fabrics or kimonos (and it wasn't an April fool's joke). When the board of directors and executives asked what would become of Takihyo, I explained, "Western clothing offers us the best promise for these changing times. The kimono is outdated, and as a Japanese business, we need to supply our consumers with the products that they desire. They need active clothing to go to work, and they need to be able to find these garments without any inconvenience. We need to move forward along with the force that is changing the way Japanese people eat, live, and think. Only with these changes can Takihyo stay ahead of the waves. If not, we will sink under the tide of the future."

Even though it had a good ring to it, this statement was purely theoretical. I had no idea how to make kimonos, but I knew just as little about making Western clothing. I had no exposure to the fashion industry before coming to Takihyo. I had learned how a business functions financially and some of the ways to put the puzzle pieces together to form a venture; however, I had no experience with implementation and application (other than my raincoat venture in Okinawa). So when the first question that the board asked me was whether I knew how to execute my plan, I could only respond, "I'll find out."

The first thing we had to do was to get rid of all of our Japanese traditional goods; thus, we sold our fabrics, kimonos, and futon covers at cost to make room for our future inventory. I also needed to find out how to make, market, and brand Western apparel—far from an easy task. The only way to do this would be for Takihyo to partner with an American company. This would allow us to learn what we needed to know about Western clothing while simultaneously generating our own revenues and offering my company some international exposure. Takihyo had plenty of cash and a solid corporate infrastructure; however, we did not have a single contact in the United States. I knew that I would have to take a gamble and take action that went against my heritage in order to make this drastic change work.

Near the end of 1961, I threw myself into the pool head first: I flew to the United States in hopes of establishing future business relationships. I had read a newspaper article citing that a company by the name of Bobbie Brooks was seeking to partner with a Japanese company in order to expand into the Far East. The Bobbie Brooks Company had been looking to establish a licensing agreement for a line of ready-to-wear clothing that was currently being sold in America. I saw the doors of opportunity open when reading this article, and I knew that I had to act fast.

I went to Cleveland, Ohio, where the Bobbie Brooks headquarters had been, and pretended to have an appointment with the late Murray Salzman—the company's president and chief executive officer (CEO). Salzman's secretary told me that I must have made a mistake and that I did not have an appointment. I brashly insisted that I did indeed; I wouldn't have flown all the way from Japan otherwise. I told her that I would be crazy to make such a move, and she agreed that "there must have been a mistake." My crazy plan worked; instead of brushing me off, Salzman welcomed me into his office.

I began the meeting by apologizing to Salzman and admitting that I lied to his secretary about having an appointment. Then I begged him to give me a few minutes of his time. I knew that he was scheduled to meet with another Japanese fashion business within the next couple of weeks; I therefore felt that he had to know how badly Takihyo needed his business and what Takihyo could offer the Bobbie Brooks company in return. I gave him a brief history of my family company and the recent changes I had implemented as the new president. I outlined my vision, and Salzman accepted the offer. Although neither he nor I was sure how well the design would work in Japan, Salzman and I entered a technical cooperation agreement to bring a subdivision of Bobbie Brooks's fashion into Japan.

By 1963, all of the details began to fall into place. The Bobbie Brooks Company had agreed to license the Stacy Ames brand to Takihyo. Although any American line would have satisfied my requirements for Takihyo becoming 100 percent Western, I was interested in the

Stacy Ames brand because it offered a new look. When my father was still alive, Takihyo had made initial forays into making Western-style clothing under the brand name Kinyo. This brand featured clothing that combined old-Japanese style with a Western sensibility. Although the line did well, the look had been quite strange. The jackets appeared to have the wide sleeves of a kimono with the cut of a Western coat around the body. More manageable and Western than a traditional kimono, this hybrid product nonetheless would not be the future of Japanese fashion. I saw a style with the Stacy Ames brand that was not only new to Japan but also innovative for the West.

The Stacy Ames clothing line had been known for its use of bonded fabrics, which eliminated the need for a lining in the garment; I thought this design showed promise. The trends began to change at Takihyo as well. Bobbie Brooks sent a team of seven to Japan to teach us how to run a Western fashion company, everything from sewing to marketing the final product. Takihyo transformed from a company that primarily wholesaled Japanese kimonos and fabrics to a company that wholesaled and manufactured women's apparel.

However, we were soon to find out that whereas manufacturing and advertising the products was one thing, wholesaling them to department stores was quite another. One of the first problems we encountered was finding a department store that would buy our Stacy Ames dresses. The buyers for Japanese stores were not very keen on taking in a brand about which they—or anyone else, for that matter—knew very little. However, after numerous negotiations, a Japanese department store called Isetan agreed to buy a limited supply of our new brand to test its value among consumers—after I pleaded for them to give Stacy Ames a chance.

Once the Stacy Ames merchandise hit the shelves, the department stores ran out of inventory within a week. The brand was an instant success. In two years, Takihyo's annual revenues skyrocketed from $30 million to $100 million (in today's dollars, a similar jump would equate to a change of about $195 million to $650 million[1]).

---

[1] See http://64.233.169.104/search?q=cache:VMTdaCjDSEJ:fx.sauder.ubc.ca/etc /USDpages.pdf+currency+exchange+historical+1960&hl=en&ct=clnk&cd=3& gl=us&client=firefox-a.

Stacy Ames was a big hit, to say the least, but it was not the only line we promoted in my first years at Takihyo. I became interested in a few other outside lines as well: Kelly Arden, Donegal, and Catalina from Kaiser Roth, to name a few. We also launched several lines within Takihyo with designs provided by a woman I hired named Dina Stern. Dina focused first on Stacy Ames, then very successfully on Kelly Arden.

Recalling the success of the raincoat factory, I wondered how I could create a line that was similar to what already existed but that used more efficient manufacturing methods to meet the demand for women's clothing. We also were paying fees for the various lines as agreed in our licensing contracts, so even though these lines did bring money into Takihyo, we had to pay large royalty fees for all of them. While mulling over this problem, I came up with a two-part solution.

First, I began experimenting with an idea that I would use later when launching one of my most successful lines after I left Japan in the early 1980s: the bridge line, also known as a type of diffusion line. Today, every major designer has a diffusion line, which essentially functions as a cash cow for the parent company. While using a similar design to the main collection, the diffusion line uses less expensive materials and has lower manufacturing costs. For instance, Donna Karan has DKNY; Ralph Lauren has Polo; and Calvin Klein has CK. However, there were no diffusion lines in the late 1960s. Designers did not create for mass distribution, but rather according to their tastes. I saw numerous avenues to recreating a look with a lower price tag.

To supersede the need to pay royalty fees, I combined the designer we hired—Dina—with the diffusion-line concept to found K2. Dina already had experience designing Stacy Ames and Kelly Arden; now we put her to work on a line wholly owned by Takihyo. K2 referred to Kelly Arden, but because the name was so different, there were no breaches of contract in the licensing agreement. However, consumers recognized both the similarity in the product lines as well as the price difference between them. Kelly Arden did not fare very well in Japan, as the line had been too expensive; however, K2 was reasonably successful. With the great success of the Stacy Ames brand, I wanted to reach other markets as well in hopes of expanding Takihyo's reach in the consumer market.

Shortly after K2, I started another line with a new Western designer; the line was called B&B: Brown and Beige. Stacy Ames had appealed to a younger audience; with this new brand I wanted clothes that would appeal to older women. B&B bridged the age gap with women's suits, half of which were knits. From 1969 until the first oil crisis in 1973, B&B did quite well.

I am proud of these accomplishments, as they were some of my first undertakings. Yet I also knew that I was still facing some very significant challenges. Takihyo was growing faster than I originally imagined it could; revenues increased 300 percent. I began to fear the company's reserves because taxes would inevitably become quite devastating if I didn't do something to offset them.

Charting the Future and Executive Drive

In his mid-20s, Tomio Taki effectively turned an already-profitable company into a far more successful one. The changes he made affected the everyday lives of both his own employees and the country's consumers. Although Tomio may have been young, he was capable of making a difference because of his capacity to see into the future and incorporate his ambition with his vision. Perhaps one of the most difficult tasks for any manager may be to accomplish this goal. That kind of drive deserves some attention.

Unlike many American managers, Tomio never claimed to be the best for the job. He recognized his flaws as a young executive who knew little about the business. However, the board rejected his desire to put his mother in the president's office—and Tomio had to learn to think differently as a result. His drive and awareness led him to make an incredibly important decision that did not only impact Takihyo's history; it also changed the way that Japanese consumers perceive fashion.

We see in Tomio, like most top executives, a need for mastery and competence. Taking the time to look through every invoice and payable shows us the dedication he has for his task.

Beyond that, I like to think of his motivational drive as an action system. What drives him is a *blending* together of the head, the heart, and the gut, and his understanding of the role and force of each. Tomio's head told him that the traditional Japanese clothing industry was a declining business. His heart asked him to reevaluate the decisions he would make and ask others for their support when he needed it. His gut allowed him to transcend Japanese normative behavior and take a huge risk by lying to Salzman's secretary. The sum of these parts made a tremendous impact on the company he would manage until his recent retirement.

Some psychologists believe that man is a creature of the physiological drive; some say he is a creature of the environment or the creature of his own mind. My position is that driven, successful executives like Tomio are constantly blending external and internal forces, each of which has an influence on behavior. I regard the head, the heart, and the gut as a single action system—one that allowed Tomio to find ways to set effective goals and to prepare himself not only for short-term gain, but as history recounts, also for the company's long-term aims. He knew how to pay attention to the details and accept his limitations as a young president. Together, these traits illustrate the psychological outline for the bright beginnings of a successful international entrepreneur.

Mortimer R. Feinberg, PhD

CHAPTER 4

A New Takihyo Headquarters
for a New Age

At only 26 years old, I shouldered a tremendous weight. Initially, I had doubted myself because I was young and inexperienced. However, as a result of hard work (and some luck), I became successful in a relatively short period of time. I owe much of this success to those who believed in me: my family, my friend at Tokai Bank, and the executives at Takihyo who forced me to take my father's place. The pressure helped push me in the right direction as well. I learned a lot by taking on such profound responsibilities.

The Stacy Ames brand helped me gain legitimacy at Takihyo. Regardless of how radical a departure this was from Takihyo's history, the change to 100 percent Western clothing brought many benefits to the company, and the line's success once again proved to me the importance of a positive outlook coupled with dedication.

However, the Western-style clothing brands couldn't be the only area in which we grew. At this point, Takihyo had much more money in pocket, and a new era had begun in Japan. These changes led me to believe that the company should expand beyond the clothing divisions, and by the mid-1960s I began to consider new business areas we could enter. So many facets of Japanese life were beginning to meld with Western practices—from the ubiquity of clothing and food to the theories underlying every aspect of the Japanese social structure. Limiting Takihyo to just clothing seemed like a mistake to me. To that end, I embarked on one of my first endeavors—a carpeting business.

Traditionally, tatami mats covered floors in Japanese homes and offices. When people entered the home or office, they removed their sandals or shoes—not only to preserve the mats but also to keep them clean. People also sat upon these mats instead of using a more Western chair. Woven from strands of grass, tatami mats had originally served as both insulators and dehumidifiers for Japanese homes and offices.

However, as Japan westernized, tatami mats were used less frequently in office spaces—desk chairs and other heavy office furniture such as filing cabinets tore the mats' lattices. As a response to the fragility of the tatami mat, Japanese started to use vinyl or linoleum floor coverings. Newer offices used linoleum because it was cheap, easy to replace, and more durable than the traditional mats. In many cases, linoleum floors were placed over tatami mats to reduce day-to-day wear and tear.

However, outside of Japan, flooring was a bit different. It seemed that others might have known something that we did not. When I traveled to the United States, I noticed that many offices had wall-to-wall carpeting. After some exposure to the new plastics that were beginning to be used in Japanese flooring, I noticed that linoleum became slick when wet. Because linoleum tended to collect dust on its surface, the slickness of the floors increased as they became dirtier. Upkeep of these kinds of floors for office spaces was quite labor intensive if this slickness was to be avoided. Nevertheless, the risk that employees would slip and injure themselves in falls was always there. I reasoned that keeping linoleum meant keeping the potential for sprained ankles and wrists. I saw how carpeting provided an inexpensive, safe, and better-looking alternative—and also a trap, rather than a collector, of airborne dust.

I decided to provide seed money from Takihyo to start a carpet company. From my perspective, I saw a niche in Japanese business that needed fulfillment. Takihyo had already been in the business of wholesaling vinyl flooring for household use. Extending Takihyo's business to include throw rugs and wall-to-wall carpeting fell in line with many of the changes since the Second World War. I started this joint venture with Mr. Wakita, a flooring specialist from the Raiko company, in the mid-1960s. We first found that the market for throw rugs had been left open, and that there was significant consumer demand.

Witnessing the great demand for throw rugs, I knew the progression to wall-to-wall would make good sense. I saw that throw rugs were not always optimal in office environments because they slip and don't cover the entire floor. Although certain high-use areas might be protected, others would wear down, thereby leaving marks and other damage to the flooring. In short, the flexibility of the throw rug was limited. With Mr. Wakita, I researched how to develop a wall-to-wall carpeting manufacturing and wholesaling business; however, this model wasn't perfect. We wanted to find materials that could offer the best and most cost-effective solution to wall-to-wall. One may think that all wall-to-wall carpeting is all the same—but it isn't. Carpets are made much like any textile—the differences in weave and materials used are vast. As a result, we found a host of problems with conventional Western-style wall-to-wall that needed attention before we could continue on our joint venture.

First, heavy furniture leaves unsightly indentations on most wall-to-wall carpeting. Using Takihyo's needs as a base for client satisfaction, I knew that the floors would look horrible after removing all of the furniture if we needed to convert a meeting or filing room into a showroom in short notice. Because filing cabinets and tables are so heavy, these indentations would be near permanent. Presentation is incredibly important in the fashion business, and if clients were to see that Takihyo did not care about how we presented our physical plant, they would likely think that we did not care about our products—which clearly wasn't an option. I was aware of the fashion industry's image-conscious nature, and knew that I had to do more research.

Wall-to-wall carpets also generate a lot of static electricity. Although it might be fun to shock a friend or partner from time to time, static gets in the way of one's productivity. After discussing these issues with a number of others and learning a bit about how carpets are manufactured, Mr. Wakita and I found a design developed by Alexander Smith that would eliminate these negatives. Smith's particular threading technique disallowed the growth of static electricity; the carpet was so tightly woven that furniture could not leave a trace. Until the second oil crisis in the late 1970s, our venture with Raiko did well in Japan.

After quadrupling the company's revenue with one of the first major forays into Western clothing and starting this carpeting joint venture, I learned that every solution generates new questions. In this case, increases in revenues meant a double-edged sword: enhanced gross profits coupled with higher taxation from the government. I knew that high tax rates would become stifling as Takihyo continued growing; thus, I needed to find a way to reduce our taxes to allow for this further future growth. Because Takihyo is such an old company and the changes I put in place had generated a lot of income, we had a large amount of cash on hand. The wave of new revenues brought in by the American designs in carpeting and fashion had compounded our earnings, and we had plenty of money to spend.

Takihyo therefore needed some kind of large depreciating asset that could also function as an investment. We had offices in Nagoya, but there were no high-rise buildings in the city at that time. Nagoya had historically been known as an industrial site. Since the late nineteenth century, some of the most forward-looking companies had started in Nagoya. For instance, Nagoya Bank, Aichi Bank, Ito Bank (which all merged to become Tokai Bank), Nagoya Gas (Toho Gas), and Okuma Machinery (Okuma Corporation) are a few examples of the city's entrepreneurial spirit that were in place well before the global empire of the Toyota Motor Corporation began. Before World War I, Nagoya was an industrial and commercial city growing at a rapid pace. During the Second World War, Allied forces razed a quarter of the city because it had been producing 60 percent of Japan's Zero fighter planes. Luckily, it didn't take long for Nagoya to rebuild after World War II—and it appeared that it would only be a matter of time before business began to grow again in the city. The demand for office space existed, and I saw a good investment in building Nagoya's first high-rise building.

Without a doubt, the demand for high-rises in the future would increase, so a building of our own would be a great asset for Takihyo. Not only would accelerated land depreciation help us with our new tax problems, but a building would also anchor our expanding company in a city poised for growth. I put in a call to a well-known construction company, Takenaka Construction, to inquire about build-ing our new headquarters. I had worked with Takenaka before. Just after the Second World War, we owned a six-story office building—the building in which I worked my first years as president. However, because most of the streets were destroyed in the war, the government had built new, uniform-sized roads across the city. In the spirit of the times, the new roads were much larger than they had been previously to accommodate streetcars and increased traffic.

The old Takihyo building had been jutting out into these new streets. The city government did not care to build around the existing structures; instead, roads were built on a grid to avoid complications for the contractors with little regard to how they were situated rela-tive to the existing buildings. The city believed that since most build-ings had been badly damaged in the war, most would end up being rebuilt anyway. However, our building was one of the few left stand-ing after the carpet bombings. Because it was made from concrete, the structure was still intact—despite most of the city having been burned to a crisp. In short, we were left with a building that not only stuck out into the street; we also had government agents knocking on our doors asking us to do something about it.

I had three options: cut the building, move the building, or raze and rebuild the building. I called in the Takenaka Construction Company to move the building—20 feet back from the street—without inter-rupting the operations. From that point forward, the construction company's president, Mr. Takenaka, became a good friend of the family. The project of moving the building took about two years, so Mr. Takenaka spent much time with our family. The Nagoya news-papers covered the building move with great interest because nothing like this had ever been done before. So much hype had been gener-ated, and so many people were curious, that the building site became a public spectacle for the two years of its moving. Sometimes people were so curious they made holes in our fencing. Because this created a security risk, we built small windows around the protective walls at three different heights: one for adults, another for children, and a third for pets. This allowed passersby both young and old to see how Takenaka ratcheted the building 20 feet back.

The building move was my first interaction with the Takenaka Construction Company, and since the project had gone so well and

I'd become friendly with the company's president, I did not hesitate to contact them again when I wanted to build a high-rise. Takenaka had a reputation for being one of the best construction companies in Japan; however, they had never built a high-rise before. Previously, Japanese zoning and building codes had not allowed high-rises because of earthquake and typhoon risks. However, architectural technologies had advanced, and the Japanese government changed the building codes to allow for high-rises.

Once these changes to the building codes were made, construction began on two new high-rises: one in Tokyo and the other in Kobe. I met with Mr. Takenaka and asked if the company were well equipped to build a high-rise. He asserted that although the technology and research had been done, the funds were not available to them yet. Because other construction companies had already begun to build high-rises, I made a move that would both uphold Takenaka's reputation as one of the top construction companies in Japan and allow me to work with Mr. Takenaka to help his company continue to build their good name: I offered the funds for the building.

The Takenaka Construction Company and Takihyo aimed to complete the high-rise quickly and inexpensively, without sacrificing any quality, thereby garnering the respect of future high-rise clients in Japan. If the building were successful, Takenaka would have a leg up on the future of Japan's construction business, as well as local business in Nagoya. In sum, building Takihyo's headquarters became more of a joint venture than a pure sponsorship. As early as the first estimates for the building, I worked closely with the Takenaka Construction Company to achieve our respective goals. I wanted to be happy with where I put my money, and I wanted the Takenaka Company to benefit from this project as well.

The Takenaka Construction and Takihyo companies also wanted to augment Nagoya city's growth as one of Japan's hubs of commerce and industry. However, constructing a building takes a long time and can be incredibly expensive. I wanted to get involved with the building's construction process as much as possible from start to finish as a businessperson protecting first Takihyo's, then Takenaka's interests.

The first directive I gave was to leave two-thirds of the lot for a park. By allowing this portion of the building's footprint to remain green, we created space for the people of the community. I felt it was important to keep in mind the human dimension in the building's design. There was a possibility that with so much heavy industry and commerce, Nagoya could transform into a dark and gloomy city without any green space. This first proposition thus yielded a two-fold gain—the people would gain a park, and Takihyo would be able to capitalize on a future trend by putting an eco-friendly spin on Nagoya's vertical climb.

The original estimates after my first discussion with Mr. Takenaka were not satisfactory. Although Mr. Takenaka's proposal had been generous compared with his competition's, I still felt it was too much since I was taking a large risk with the inexperience of his company in building these types of buildings. I wanted to help. I looked over the numbers and found that the largest single cost was for lifting raw materials. After constructing the building's skeleton, workers below would lift materials to workers above. Although many other construction companies employed this method, I found it incredibly inefficient and thought that it wasted both time and money.

Because building a high-rise is dangerous for the workers who assemble parts of the building so many stories up, labor costs must provide ample incentive for workers to risk life and limb. Yet even if the pay is significantly higher, plenty of these workers would still opt *not* to do the job for fear of falling. In addition, no one would be working on the building if the wind were blowing too hard or if it were raining; safety concerns would inevitably cause delays. In sum, building a high-rise the way Takenaka intended entailed putting people at risk, raising costs, and slowing down the project.

With an eye toward both financial and safety concerns, I wanted to use my knowledge of manufacturing efficiencies to develop a new method for building that would not only decrease the number of hours spent stories above and lifting costs associated (thereby lowering my bottom line as a sponsor) but would also help Takenaka find safer and faster ways to accomplish his aims *without* sacrificing the quality of the project.

I quickly realized it would be far more efficient to construct the building in stages on the ground and lift each preassembled segment to workers stories above. The architects agreed and devised a plan to assemble the facades of the building in panels 40 feet wide and 9 feet tall. They would build three-floor units first, constructing them safely on the ground rather than many stories in the air. These changes shrank lifting costs and time by 80 percent without sacrificing the building's structural integrity. These innovations—which saved hundreds of millions of yen—enabled the project to finish a year in advance and under budget—and created a work site that was drastically safer than any of Takenaka's competitors.

Before the building's completion, I began designing the interior. Although I could use Takihyo's own carpets to lay wall-to-wall, I wanted to otherwise soften the rigid structure of traditional Japanese office space into something that would still be manageable. I needed a modular office solution. Versatility in the office space was paramount for me. I wanted my furniture and walls to facilitate any temporary changes in the space. When I looked to the United States for a furniture/office systems company, Steelcase caught my eye.

Mr. Jim Wo, my good friend from Hawaii who was in the furniture business, introduced me to the management of Steelcase in Grand Rapids, Michigan. Steelcase was attractive because of the mobility of its office systems. The best utilization of space seemed to be that which offered the most flexibility with furniture. At times, Takihyo needed more space for a showroom, and at other times, more space for desks. Although Herman Miller designed the ultra-portable office system, Steelcase had been the first to capitalize on it—mass-producing Miller's ingenuity. What made this system so much better than the others was the fact that all the walls were light and mobile. They were constructed of panels that could be moved and configured to fit any kind of space—square, rectangular, octagonal, you name it. The panels included telephone and electrical wiring and a fluorescent light that would illuminate from the top against the ceiling to provide indirect light. This kind of light was particularly appealing because of its softness, which made a big difference in office productivity. I—as well as many others—found it easier to concentrate with indirect light rather than glaring fluorescent bulbs.

However, I knew that it would be impossible to ship the office systems from the United States to Japan. The costs would be too high, and it simply would not be worth it considering how much we needed. I reasoned that if Steelcase agreed to license their manufacturing technique to a company in the Far East, Takihyo could buy locally. Having little knowledge of the furniture business, I turned to my friend Mr. Jiro Ushio, who introduced me to Susumu Kodaira, president of the Japanese furniture wholesaler Mobilia. I asked Mr. Kodaira if he would be interested in a joint venture with the American company and he agreed. I told him I would be flying to Grand Rapids the following week.

My next move was to find a manufacturer in Japan, but I had less than a week before my meeting with the Steelcase executives. What made matters a bit more complex was the fact that neither Kodaira nor I had a connection to a manufacturer who could reproduce Steelcase's designs. After conducting a little research, Kodaira and I found three companies that could possibly accommodate our needs. One in particular seemed to offer the best fit for us: a company called Kurogane.

I called Kurogane and asked for the president. His secretary told me he was not in the office and wasn't going to return until the following week. Because we were also in the process of completing the building, I did not have a week. Takihyo needed functional offices to continue running our company. After a few more calls, we went to the general affairs office and I told them I had something very important to deliver to the president. Although I learned that he was sick and in the hospital, they gave me all of the information I needed to find him.

Kurogane's president did not have any serious ailments or injuries; he had simply been in the hospital for some annual testing. I called to let him know that I was coming to his room to propose a joint venture with Steelcase to build the furniture for Takihyo's new building and offer the same products to other companies. He said that he could not give me an answer at that time and asked for a week to think about it. I knew that I didn't have a week to wait on a possible "no." I told him that if he did not have a definite answer for me the following day, I would solicit a contract from one of his competitors. I got a call the following day confirming our business partnership. Shortly thereafter, Mr. Kodaira and I met with the Steelcase executives and sealed the deal.

I am not a pushy guy in my personal life; in fact, I try to step on as few toes as possible. When it comes to business, however, there are times that I know I need to put pressure on other people. My fear in this particular scenario was that the decision-making process would be delayed for too long. Because of the pressures I was under, I had to turn up the heat while offering fair deals under the serious time constraints Takihyo faced.

Getting Others to See Things Your Way

Although this chapter provides a number of interesting points from a managerial perspective, I find the most intriguing as a psychologist to be Tomio Taki's ability to persuade Takenaka and Kurogane's president using both reason and hard negotiating tactics. Tomio knew what stimulated the executives he targeted; he was also aware of the proposals that would have left those same executives cold. For those wondering how Tomio accomplished these feats, consider the following insight into business psychology:

Whenever you advance an idea, a plan, a proposal, or a program that you want to be adopted, you must take into account the individuality of the people who compose your audience—and consider the kind of people you're dealing with. For example—Tomio knew that the Kurogane president would sit in his hospital bed and think about the deal he was offered for what would feel like an eternity, even though it would be only one day. Tomio was aware of the pressure he had put on this executive; he knew that an outcome would be well deliberated.

Bear in mind the democratic process when you're addressing such problems. Is it possible to give your people a choice in scenarios like these and weigh individuality? Whenever there is an option—and people receive the opportunity to choose according to their individuality—the chances of winning their support grow exponentially. This matter of individual differences is basic to the whole subject of persuasion; in many respects, it is basic to life itself.

Selling an idea or a plan is always better than debating over it. Watch a good salesperson operate. Study some examples of good advertising. Do you see any debates in these forms of selling? If you do, then chances are that the sales pitch isn't too effective.

You perform the same kind of sales activity as if you were selling vacuum cleaners or cosmetics when you attempt to persuade someone to do something. The only difference is that you are selling an *attitude* instead of a product or service; therefore, you can apply the basic principles of selling with good results. In fact, when it comes to persuasion, you might even improve on the standard sales technique. Whereas top salespeople prefer to never mention the competition, psychological research shows that you stand to gain by using the competition in persuasion.

This is precisely what Tomio did with the Kurogane executive by anticipating the opinions and reactions of others. Typically, if you can anticipate a negative reaction to your proposal, you want to address it quickly—and proceed to make a strong case for yourself. If Tomio knew that someone would take the bait, he could easily move on. Because he offered a good deal for the Kurogane executive, he might have known that the deal was in the bag. Tomio felt as though he didn't even need to make a case for himself, because his initial proposal was so fair.

Studies show that you have not really sold your case if you present only your side. That's because your audience will be more easily unconvinced when they hear the other side than they might have been had they initially heard both sides from you. In other words, if you think that your audience originally heard, knows of, or will eventually hear the arguments against you, it is very much worth it to devote some time to the opposition. Give your audience some mental ammunition with which to defend the position you hope they'll take.

It will also be to your advantage to anticipate the opposition if your audience is intelligent and sophisticated enough to look for flaws in your argument. Moreover, if you don't *impress* an intelligent audience by your knowledge of the competition, they may lose respect for you and your case. As Tomio has recounted in this chapter, you have to beat your audience to its own best punch.

(continued)

(continued)

However, there are also some limitations to the methods that Tomio employed in this chapter. Pushing for immediate compliance, as Tomio did, sometimes works in selling when you want a man to put his name on the dotted line (as it was in Tomio's case). But in most other situations, this kind of urge for immediate compliance will not have lasting results. It is okay if you are trying to inspire a man for the moment; however, if you want to convince someone to change long-held habits or attitudes, don't demand immediate action. Give the person a chance to think it over.

One risk that comes with asking for an immediate answer is the possibility that others may later think they have been hoodwinked, tricked, or conned—which means that all your persuasive effort will have gone for naught. Of course, you don't have to wait indefinitely for an answer. Set a timetable for decision and opinion making while permitting someone to mull over your argument. For example, if you are asking a subordinate to consider a transfer, give that person a few days to ponder the possibilities and discuss them with his or her spouse or partner. Whatever the employee's eventual decision, chances are the subordinate will be happier with it—and so will you.

Granting someone a short "think it over" period before asking for a commitment also gives that person the chance to vent any emotions. Individuals may need an opportunity to get things off their chest; they may come to you with some very real (at least to them) objections to your proposal. Watch them carefully; you may learn something that will give you an advantage. You may be able to find out what is *really* bothering them, which means that now you will direct your future persuasive efforts directly at a specific target. Consequently, you can persuade more effectively.

I once met a top executive who frequently negotiates mergers. So doing, he invokes the "do not push for immediate compliance" principle. He always starts by knowing that he will take his time and determine what it is about the merger that appeals or does not appeal to his adversary. Maybe the other party wants money. Maybe it's security. Maybe the other person's spouse wants something. At any rate, this man never rushes negotiations until he is positive about the other party's goals and is prepared to make an offer along these lines. "If I push too early without knowing the real target," he told me, "it results in an intellectual exercise rather than a deal."

The last point I would like to make regards the importance of sincerity in any negotiation or persuasive effort. The impression you make depends on a whole series of past impacts on the people with whom you're interacting. You must build a general background of sincerity, rather than try to pull something off on the spur of the moment.

The one thing you do not wish to convey when you persuade people is the very fact that you are persuading them. Once someone believes that you are manipulating him or her, that person begins to mistrust you. The individual begins to wonder what's in it for you; what do you have to gain personally?

No one takes notes on every little act you perform and reviews them in an attempt to judge your sincerity whenever you show up with persuasion on your mind. But a consecutive, consistent series of simple transactions, all performed honestly in the name of sincerity, will eventually total up to a nice sincere image of you. And developing such a reputation will always give you an advantage.

Mortimer R. Feinberg, PhD

CHAPTER 5

Expansion and Distribution Channel Management

The Late 1960s

I was fortunate enough to experience mostly advantages during the first 14 years of my business career and personal life. I had a wife and healthy twin boys, and Takihyo was growing at a tremendous pace. The side projects of licensing for Steelcase, the construction of the Takihyo headquarters in Nagoya, Takihyo's licensing of Bobbie Brooks's Stacy Ames brand, and our carpeting wholesaling division were more lucrative than I initially imagined they could be. With the introduction of these new lifestyle-marketed items, women's Western clothing, and household goods, Takihyo embarked on changing from the old into the new. However, as the company evolved, so did the consumer—requiring us to adapt to a much more sophisticated consumer with new methods of distribution and marketing.

Takihyo needed a new distribution hub to expand and accommodate new demand. Although it is common practice today, Japanese businesses did not at that time have separate distribution centers. It was not until I'd traveled to the United States that I noticed how essential a distribution center would be for Takihyo. These centers allowed more room in the office to be devoted to desks and showrooms, rather than

51

having to store boxes upon boxes of samples and products. On-site storage took away from our productivity in the office, because we were forced to spend too much time contracting messengers to ship samples and products rather than focusing on running the business. In other words, we were getting bogged down managing operational logistics when we should have been managing task delegation.

A new distribution center would also reduce costs as the company developed. As Nagoya grew, real estate values rose. I realized that by using a large portion of my headquarters as storage, I was ignoring the increase in the per-square-meter price of real estate. If the distribution hub were located somewhere else—specifically, somewhere with lower real estate values—the high price per meter would be suited better for people than for materials or products.

So I started a new company—a distribution center to manage incoming and outgoing inventory. I wanted those closest to the products to manage them. Initially, buyers in Japan were skeptical about the idea. When it came to fashion, they wanted to be able to see and touch everything on-site instead of making deals without seeing a significant percentage of the samples. In time, however, the new company—which I named Chu-Bu Distribution Center—streamlined Takihyo's distribution management.

But our growth and development could not stop there. Not only was business changing, so too were our customers in every arena. The nation's pulse grew faster and stronger—and consumers were yearning for distinct ways to express their individuality.

The distribution center had to provide Takihyo with a means to bring the right products to the right places. Typically, we were selling goods to department stores and various wholesalers, but this was before individuality determined the flow of our products. Our new clientele had differing tastes, and some held an allegiance to one store over the other. The vision behind the Chu-Bu Distribution Center focused on how to supply the right marketplaces with the right goods. The new chain-store concept spread like wildfire in Japan in the late 1960s. Previously, there had been only department stores, specialty stores, and mom-and-pop boutiques—all of which were destination locations. Each offered a particular brand of merchandise that could only be found there. Department stores even went out of their way to offer amenities to shoppers to keep them there longer and hopefully acquire a few more sales in the process. Some of these amenities were expensive for department stores to offer, but revenues from garment sales would tip the scales positively. Specialty stores always served a niche market; they would continue to do so as long as their products did not become so commonly used that everyone wanted what they had to offer and a bigger player steped in to provide it. (Mom-and-pop stores, though, did not fare as well; they could not compete as well against chain stores, and many disappeared.) Since chain stores were one of our customers, we needed to find a way to help them as well as ourselves in this new, challenging environment.

Chain stores differed from department stores in their relative convenience and the types of goods they sold. Chain stores would open a large number of locations, all selling the same goods to the masses, whereas many department stores would have only one or two locations. Chain stores also grew more aware of how branding could persuade their consumers to buy one product over another. It had previously been only the department stores that worried about how lighting could affect a sale; now, newer chain stores were more interested in merchandising their product properly. Takihyo even played a key role in forming one chain store company, called Jusco. However, before I describe how Jusco came about, I should provide some context about the competitive environment at the time.

I saw massive holes in how chain stores were operating in those years. There were two major players in Japan: Daiei and Seiyu. Daiei developed from a drugstore chain into a general merchandise, full-scale chain store and sold all kinds of goods including foodstuffs. Seiyu was more like a convenience store or kiosk and had been established by Seibu Railroad Company as a general merchandise chain store, initially as a way to generate extra revenues along the rail routes.

Stores like Seiyu and Daiei took a very simple approach: they bought merchandise, displayed it on the shelves, and sold it in bulk. They tried to keep overhead low so that they could offer merchandise to the consumer at a lower price. Although this business model worked well for Seiyu and Daiei, there were no general merchandise chain stores at the time that sold clothing—and it was only a matter of time before the chain-store trend would hit fashion for the masses. I felt that it was only natural at this point to start a conversation with Mr. Okada, a chain-store executive from Osaka. After numerous dinners and talks,

I convinced Mr. Okada to merge, with Takihyo's help, three up-and-coming chain stores in Japan: Okadaiya, Futagi, and Shiro.[1] Okadaiya and Futagi had been chain stores based in other cities.

Daiei and Seiyu were doing quite well. So from an outside standpoint—looking solely at financial statements—these companies owned the chain store niche. However, the concept of the Jusco chain store fit somewhat outside of what those mega-chain stores were already offering. Stores like Daiei and Seiyu never dealt with fashion, nor did they understand how to market in that industry. Layouts were not important to them; they did nothing to create added value for their products. Items were merely stacked on shelves or tables, and consumers were expected to search through the items to find what they wanted. There was little to no organization; the idea was just too simple, I thought, for the new Japanese shopping public. Their approach was too rough around the edges. I knew that Jusco could bridge the gap between department stores and what people had come to think of as the chain store.

Modern concepts of design separated the new Jusco stores from the other chain stores. Jusco offered food, clothing, and the same convenience store items in one place like some of the others; but because we had some background knowledge in retail and merchandising, Jusco's stores were easier to navigate and much more consumer-friendly to clothing shoppers. By organizing the clothes by type and brand, we managed to establish an atmosphere that strengthened the core of the business. We wanted to highlight certain items while making others accessible in the same market. Jusco would therefore offer a number of options; however, management would make clear, conscious decisions about what pieces would be merchandised best to show variety for the consumer in a fashion-conscious way.

Although building a new distribution channel for Takihyo's goods was our main goal, our efforts had additional results. The birth of the chain store had given rise to a whole new set of problems. Department stores were less interested in buying goods from large wholesalers because their profit margins shrank with each hand in the deal; therefore, department stores wanted direct access to manufacturers.

---

[1]Shiro is a supermarket chain based in Osaka.

This movement threatened some of our business, so I strove to find a solution—not only to keep relationships with department stores alive but also to grow new ones, such as with the Jusco chain stores. The new distribution company played an integral role in this process as I had to force Takihyo to adopt a new distribution channel management system.

More specifically, the chain stores would allow us to wholesale or manufacture certain kinds of garments; another set of garments would be directed to specialty stores; and a third type would go to department stores. Each type would sell different goods at different price points: we wanted to sell our goods at all of them. Geography would also dictate what we would sell where. Some mom-and-pop stores would receive the same items a chain store would, but on the other side of the country and vice versa. Although I knew that the chain stores could provide Takihyo with a strong source of revenue, we wanted to keep business with the department stores as well; therefore, we formed new relationships with manufacturers across Japan. Our goal had always been to become a kind of one-stop wholesale shop with total manufacturing capabilities. Department stores would receive the kinds of products their consumers wanted, whereas chain stores and smaller boutiques would get entirely different sets. Demands and demographics also differed greatly depending on the type of store, so I pushed Takihyo's manufacturing and wholesaling capabilities to meet these demands. There was no other way to grow in this kind of environment without outside thinking and help.

One reason for these divisions arose from the ways in which department stores marketed themselves as compared with chain stores or boutiques. A consumer's trip across the city simply to visit the department store could be justified by the fact that the specific product the consumer was looking for could be found only at that store. The product's specialness was therefore what became important; the kinds of items we could sell to department stores needed to adapt to a dynamic consumer base. Chain stores tended to sell basics; therefore, customers tended to be a bit more static in their needs. Department stores, on the other hand, were geared more to selling fashion and merchandising the products so they looked sexy.

The items sold at chain stores are more often than not tonnage or high-volume merchandise. If a chain store had many locations in a small area, all of the stores would sell more or less the same merchandise, thereby offering the consumer geographical convenience and a static base of product offerings. This allowed chain stores' margins to remain low and let them be less brand conscious than department stores. For a fuller view, consider the key concept that was budding in my mind at the time: emotional value.

My favorite example of a piece of clothing with emotional value is the necktie. Neckties serve no purpose other than hanging on your neck. They're made from very little fabric, and labor costs are proportionately low. However, some ties sell for as much as an inexpensive suit or dress. Their color, pattern, fabric, and brand can dictate what prices the consumers will pay. A well-respected or widely known brand may sell a T-shirt and a tie for the same price. A company such as BVD or Limited Brands' Victoria's Secret may sell a product that's similar to that of a high-end designer company's, perhaps even made from the same materials in the same factory.

However, the price point and gross margin may diverge significantly due to the way consumers—and entire markets—view Victoria's Secret versus the way they perceive a high-end design house. The BVDs and Victoria's Secrets of the world sell in volume with small gross margins and thus pay little mind to the enhanced value a couture brand name may offer—thereby adding little emotional value to a product. Then again, companies such as BVD and Victoria's Secret sell items that people *need*—not something that they want. A brand-name necktie may also justify its price based on the fact that neckties are a bigger risk for the brand and the manufacturers than underwear. Regardless of pricing and margins, a product's emotional value is influenced by a whole slew of factors ranging from celebrity sponsorship and enticing advertisements to lighting in a store or placement of a garment on a mannequin.

Moreover, emotional value stems from any added layer of creativity, regardless of the source. If designer A makes a cashmere dress that has a fantastic design and designer B makes a dress from the same fabric but that is a bit less interesting, then designer A's dresses are sure to sell out long before designer B's—if both dresses are selling at the same price. Absent any other mitigating factors, better or trendier design will always be more popular—and thus more successful. However, creativity in fashion design doesn't always take the cake when it comes to emotional value; sometimes slapping on a name brand works just as well.

In any case, design exists in everything everywhere. There is nothing in this world that is created that doesn't have some kind of aesthetic inclination or reference to the potential of the human hand.

Another example of a way to enhance the emotional value of a particular store—and the brands within it—is through merchandising. Although it's a very different approach than enhancing emotional value, a creative and consumer-friendly merchandising method can change what does and does not sell.

The tactics used in merchandising can create significant emotional connections in any retail setting. One particular area that has had a particular effect on consumers is lighting; it plays an incredibly important role in selling. If a consumer is able to select a product more effectively because of enhanced visibility, then the chances of making the sale are that much greater. Consumers do not want to have to search for something; they want it right at the moment that they want it. If searching costs the consumer an extra 10 minutes, frustration may set in—which could possibly result in shoppers leaving dissatisfied and without having bought anything. For this reason, I wanted to design the Jusco stores with a bit of an edge over other chain stores—and even over department stores, which offered the same products as chain stores but their products were easier to find and arranged more attractively.

In any business, particularly in retail, the consumer should remain the focal point from the beginning to the end of the distribution chain: starting with those selling raw materials and finishing with those retailing the finished product. Changing the way in which you light a product and bringing food into the shopping experience offer two very different approaches to working with the consumer's viewpoint.

Lighting has the potential to change an item's desirability. Because it can recreate dimensionality, changes in lighting are a simple way to make a huge difference in how consumers see products. As already stated, consumers don't want to work to find something—which makes floor layout and organization a primary concern for stores. However, retailers don't always have an eye for this kind of setup; they often need additional help. For example, a garment on a hanger is a two-dimensional image—regardless of the quality, fit, color, size, shape—and is less appealing than a three-dimensional image, which can be simulated by broadly lighting dressed mannequins and placing them strategically to catch the eyes of wandering consumers.

Creating a scene in which mannequins wear the garments provides consumers with a more objective perspective as to how the clothing will look on them. Showing clothing in this way offers retailers and wholesalers a proverbial layup to selling a product: if they showcase the most beautiful pieces in this way, they will surely gain the attention deserved. Meanwhile, similar designs from the same line will be given more consumer credibility. A clean layout will offer a sense of comfort to the shopping experience while allowing retailers and merchandisers to have some control over the consumer's physical movement and visual space.

Another way in which I added emotional value to the chain-store concept at Jusco was with food. Not until the last 30 years or so have stores sold food and offered a place where consumers could rest and relax before either heading home or continuing their errands. Most of the time, a consumer's only option if he or she became hungry—or tired from walking—was to return home. However, linking eating with shopping gives consumers more time to peruse—which then increases the potential for another sale and another satisfied customer. I was able to implement this idea after pushing it with the Jusco executives—and the positive effects showed on the profit and loss statements.

Altering the way in which a consumer shops and experiences shopping by making it far more convenient and comfortable had been my underlying goal in helping to establish Jusco. Takihyo needed to form some new connections, and a fresh look at the chain-store concept gave us a push to take further control over one area of Japan's new set of distribution chains. I felt that we needed more control over all aspects of the shopping experience in order to move forward and keep pace with an emerging consciousness of the individual that was affecting areas ranging from politics to fashion in Japan during the late 1960s. I wanted Takihyo to be ahead of the curve—finding methods of retailing and merchandising that had never before existed in Japan.

By taking some American ideas from what I'd noticed overseas and incorporating them with some of my own, I learned that the increasing complexity of the garment business meant one thing: I would have to change too. More important, the then-200-year-old Takihyo would have to alter its processes and approaches to succeed in this much more demanding market. Our ability to manage shoppers' various needs and demands (by properly lighting and placing products, for example, and offering food and a place to rest) not only enhanced their shopping experience but also improved customers' lifestyles by promoting their convenience and comfort while at the same time padding our profit margins.

A trained eye will always be able to see the emotional value that's added to the material value of a product that's well merchandised. The material value of the product—costs—is different from the emotional value. The difference is evident in how design houses add emotional value to their products. Adding emotional value to a store's space, however, is quite different. Both chain stores and department stores have to attract consumers. How they sell the goods and amenities they offer represents different modes of convenience. Chain stores tend to position themselves for the shopper's convenience, whereas department and specialty stores tend to be a destination shopping location. The difference between entering a CVS drugstore and entering a Saks Fifth Avenue department store is quite stark and represents customers' shifting priorities. Coming to grips with these ideas helped Takihyo thrive in the late 1960s.

Making Yourself More Creative

There are people who say that creativity is a miracle of nature, that it just happens for certain lucky individuals. Tchaikovsky once compared creative compositions to an act of nature: "If the soil is ready, the germ of a future composition takes root with extraordinary force and rapidity, shoots up through the earth, puts forth branches, leaves and finally blossoms." However, creativity, in its simplest and most usual form, is really only a variation of problem solving. It is little more than an exercise in attacking a mental challenge.

(continued)

(continued)

We saw in this chapter how Tomio Taki mapped the minds of consumers as he was able to break down ways in which he could add emotional value to products. He derived his methods from personal experience and took the time to analyze the different components that he knew he had to take to heart when structuring the new Jusco chain stores in Japan. He combined his insights with a particular mind for making the business better—not only for the companies' income but also to satiate the consumers' differing demands. The packaging of prepared foods offers a great example of how Tomio thought outside of the box to make a successful venture more intuitive to the needs of consumers.

So what does this creative process entail? Is it only limited to those who are radical by nature, or can we all apply Tomio's methods to our own situations?

If you were to take the creative process apart and analyze its components, you would find that there are always four stages in developing creative thought. First, there is preparation. This is the stage in which you come to recognize the problem or mental challenge—how to make the product or store better for the consumer, for example. It involves learning what must be accomplished and may consist of a formal approach that involves lengthy investigation and discussions. On the other hand, it may be merely a general awareness, such as the need to rearrange items in a store to make them more accessible and easier to find. A manager's background and experience offer some preparation for creative problem solving.

The second stage, incubation, takes place when the mind appears to be inactive but is in reality turning over all the possibilities in the unconscious. People are usually not even aware of what is going on inside their minds, since they're frequently engaged in other activities at the time. Patience is a virtue during this stage, as producing a new idea may take anywhere from a matter of seconds to years.

Illumination is the third stage when the mind comes up with that innovation. It may be the basic solution to your problem, or perhaps it is the insight you need to open up a whole new field of thought. Sometimes this illumination comes suddenly; things just seem to fall into place. You may jump up in the middle of the night with the idea you've waited weeks or months to come to you.

The last stage in the creative process is verification. This is the process of refining the idea and determining if it works, and this requires a period of judgment and decision making.

I have observed that executives are, generally speaking, more creative in some of these stages than others. I have seen many executives who simply cannot come up with a new idea but who are great when it comes to separating the good ideas from the bad. Some managers are effective sifters of solutions to problems; they are critics who can do wonderful things when it comes to promoting and merchandising ideas. Yet many of these kinds of thinkers may be hard pressed to come up with ideas themselves.

There are some very definite reasons why particular people aren't more creative, and most of these reasons fall into two broad but well-defined categories: psychological and perceptual. There are several subcategories among the psychological reasons why someone may not be creative. These blocks have their justifications, but they nevertheless cause problems when it comes to creative thinking.

It takes time to develop a new idea. It is much more expedient to go along with what is presently being done than to develop a totally new approach. Therefore, most executives in business and industry simply do not have the time to study problems and to permit their minds the luxury of wandering through the four steps we just discussed. It also takes a thick skin to come up with new ideas, because it frequently requires being open to the fact that others might reject them.

Many people who develop new ideas are regarded as oddballs— and I lovingly include Tomio Taki in this category. Perhaps Tomio's tough but most formative years during World War II provided

(continued)

(continued)

him with the toolbox he needed to become as successful as he is. A creative manager has to expose himself to harsh critical judgment. Other executives criticized Tomio for wanting to transform Takihyo into a wholesaler and manufacturer of Western clothing. Sometimes, other people's evaluation of new ideas takes the form of ridicule, satire, and personal degradation. It takes courage to propose new notions and then to expose both the ideas and yourself to potential dismissal. This part of the creative process requires quite a bit of dedication and commitment.

Eventually, every creative person encounters some hostility. No one has ever come up with a new, worthwhile idea without encountering opposition from people who believed 100 percent in the old idea and refused to accept the new. We all know people who hold their own ideas as sacred. Thus, to sell your new idea and see that it wins acceptance, you have to be totally committed to it. After all—how can you convince others of its merit if you aren't?

The last psychological block for creativity takes place when one's status is threatened. Suppose, for example, that you go to great extremes to develop, propose, or sell a fresh approach to a nagging problem. Everyone stakes his all on you—and your approach turns out to be a total failure. It flops. How does this affect your reputation? Certainly, it has come down a notch or two.

The term *perceptual blocks* refers to the way in which certain previously held frames of reference can keep you from looking at an old problem from a new angle. In the immensely popular film *Die Hard with a Vengeance* starring Bruce Willis as John McClane and Samuel L. Jackson as Zeus Carver, the two men are forced to solve a classic mathematics problem that exemplifies how to get around a perceptual block. McClane and Carver must place exactly 4 quarts of water onto a scale which would then deactivate the ticking time bomb in a public park. The problem, however, is that both McClane and Carver were given only 5-quart and 3-quart jugs, which were placed by a public water fountain near the bomb.

If the film's antagonist had given them four 1-quart jugs, McClane and Carver could easily solve this challenge. But the 5- and 3-quart jugs force the two to use their rational problem-solving skills to dismantle the bomb. The solution they came to was as follows: first fill the 5-quart jug with water and then dump 3 quarts of the water into the 3-quart jug, leaving 2 quarts of water in the 5-quart jug. The empty 3-quart jug was then filled with the 2 quarts from the 5-quart jug. The 3-quart jug then had 2 quarts of water and the 5-quart jug was empty. Filling up the 5-quart jug, then pouring the water into the 3-quart jug until that jug was full, left the 5-quart jug holding exactly 4 quarts of water.

So what does this example from Hollywood teach us? In the business world, you can't afford to let the wrong frame of reference take you the long way 'round. Personal success depends on your ability to break away from the common perspective and find the better—often shorter—and more lucrative way. The kind of problem solving that McClane and Carver underwent is similar to the problem-solving skills that managers need to undergo while preparing and implementing the kind of creative thinking that leads to innovative solutions.

Although there may be numerous ways to break a flawed frame of reference, there are two measures you can take to overcome perceptual barriers when problem solving. The first is to turn the problem upside down by asking questions such as: What if this situation—and the cause and effect therein—were reversed? If it's horizontal, suppose it were vertical? If vertical, suppose it were horizontal? If it's long, suppose it were short? If short, long; if high, low; if inside, outside; if it were on top, suppose it were on the bottom?

Henry Ford used this technique successfully to create the assembly line. All industrialists were looking for ways to bring employees to the materials and production area. Ford reversed his thinking by bringing the production area and materials to the employees. The idea of the assembly line emerged and later became the basis of mass production.

(continued)

(continued)

The second thing you can do to overcome perceptual barriers is to challenge your assumptions. Say it isn't so. Columbus, Hudson, Magellan, and other explorers challenged what everyone was taking for granted and opened up a whole new world of discovery for Western Europe. Pasteur challenged assumptions in medicine, Einstein in physics, Nash in economics and game theory. In challenging assumptions that clouded and restricted others, these men found new paths to better ideas.

Asking the right questions helps move this process along: Does it have to be this way? Does it have to be done here? We've always taken this approach; why not do something different? In this chapter Tomio described how he revolutionized the way that consumers could shop; during this process, Tomio thought about the different factors that come into play on a daily basis. For example, people need to eat, and people like to shop. So he brought the two together. When a shopper doesn't have much time and is in a hurry but hungry, picking up something light and fast is a great option. Tomio broke the frame of reference by challenging the assumption that fresh food that couldn't be displayed needed to be thrown away, rather than resold in a packaged form. Coming up with real-world solutions may simply derive from posing questions about the fundamentals.

Mortimer R. Feinberg, PhD

CHAPTER 6

Taki Gakuen and Asking the Simple Questions

In 1928 my grandfather, Nobushiro Taki, established Taki Gakuen, a school near his hometown. His mission was to educate the countryside. He yearned to develop sophisticated and well-versed farmers as well as businessmen. The school had two primary curricula—agricultural and business courses—to accommodate the needs of local students. The school's funding derived from my grandfather's investments in Korean chestnut and apple farms, as well as a substantial interest in the Northern Manchurian Railroad. The fruits of these business interests allowed Taki Gakuen to offer local students almost tuition-free matriculation to our private institution.

My father assumed responsibility for the school when my grandfather passed away. After this shift, the end of the Second World War ushered in a wave of new problems. The school's financial stability was challenged for the first time in its history as the Korean government claimed that the school's farmlands were in Korea and the Northern Manchurian Railroad was usurped. The Korean property went under the control of the UN and Inner Manchuria was returned to the Republic of China. This return of property caused a great deal

of fiscal strain on the school that my father had to address. For the
time my father was in charge, he did his best to maintain my grandfather's vision while beginning to adapt the school to a more modern pedagogical approach. However, everything was turned upside
down again when my father passed away unexpectedly. With the
torch then passed to me, I was forced to confront these problems
with even fewer available resources.

In a short time, I had to make a number of quick business decisions
to keep the school afloat. After careful investigation, I found that the
two curricula weren't working. From the 1930s until the 1950s and
1960s, we witnessed many social and environmental changes, particularly in the suburbs of Nagoya. Developers rezoned and built on top
of what was once farmland to create housing to accommodate bur-
geoning demand. Students didn't want to learn how to farm now, so
this curriculum no longer fit the region's demographics. As a result,
the agricultural program was very costly to maintain. The faculty/
staff-to-student ratio was approximately 12 to 5. The teachers we
had consisted of breeding specialists and all different kinds of
veterinarians—doctors whose educations demanded a higher pay scale
than liberal arts teachers with master's degrees. There was no upside
to supporting the agricultural division, so I decided to shut it down.

When my grandfather established Taki Gakuen, Nagoya had yet
to industrialize in the way it did just before and during the Second
World War. This city was a region of local farmers then. The soil had
been rich and fertile because the land had once rested at the bottom
of a river bed. In fact, the land had once been used to meet most of
the agricultural needs of the surrounding areas. However, the presence of industry mushroomed. Increasing numbers of light industries
began to populate the area and agriculture began a steady decline. By
the Second World War, Nagoya was renowned for heavy industry—
particularly in the manufacturing of airplanes and cars. The paradigm
shift that occurred in the city made teaching agriculture nonsensical.

Although my father had added a college-prep curriculum during
his administration, this program was not attracting the deserved attention. We had very few applicants when I took over the school, so each
senior faculty and staff member was forced to recruit family and friends
to enroll for the first couple of years. Even though word of mouth is
often the best form of advertising, it wasn't working in this particular

instance. There just wasn't enough demand, and the school needed a new philosophy. So I sought other ways to transform the institution.

I knew that increasing the number of applications and improving the quality of education would go hand-in-hand. Being able to gain Taki Gakuen's students admission into the best colleges and universities would build the reputation we were seeking. With that as our goal, I saw avenues of necessary improvement for the school: a superior faculty and a robust, comprehensive curriculum. I started a new hiring initiative that centered on searching for the most capable teachers, rather than those with a fancy résumé. From my experience as a beneficiary of Japan's best schooling, I had learned that no matter how brilliant a scholar, there are other elements that make someone a brilliant teacher.

I ordered the deans and assistant deans to hire seasoned, experienced teachers and offer them 50 percent more than the salaries they were making at their current institutions. I dropped the business curriculum and focused more on a liberal arts education—the courses found in modern preparatory schools. This pedagogy seemed more appropriate and advantageous to our students' future. I reasoned that the entire school should become a model prep school for the region.

My next approach was subjective. I asked myself as a parent and a consumer what *I* and others would want from a school. The answer was fairly simple: to make Taki Gakuen the best option for the most applicants. If good universities and colleges accepted Taki Gakuen's students, the alumni body would become that much stronger, and the number of future opportunities would grow each year for every graduate. Some distinguished graduates would return to Taki Gakuen to discuss their successes, which would uplift the morale of both students and parents. In addition, students would learn about different career options from these talks and gain inspiration from those who had realized their own dreams. My mission was to instill hope backed by motivation, ambition, and diligence.

After I'd planned and executed the school's rescue plan, the situation at Taki Gakuen dramatically improved. Today, the school sends some of the brightest and best of Japan to top colleges and universities. The foundations of this story echo my theory of management; this is the reason I bring this anecdote to light. Because I was more interested in interacting with the school as a business that had customers who were demanding satisfaction, I could accomplish my aims. I wanted to run the school as a better company—one that offered the best products and services.

Creating new means to sell the school to parents, however, was easier for me than reorganizing the school. In the traditional Japanese corporate world, the company is your family. In many cases, the company's needs can take precedence over the employee's family's emotional needs. The company hires an employee and learns his or her strengths and weaknesses; then the managers train and place the employee in the position best suited to his or her skill set. Although Japanese corporate culture is changing, one thing remains the same: in a traditional company, you are never fired once you're hired. In other words, the shift in pedagogical implementation addressed only one of the problems the school was facing. After closing the agricultural division at Taki Gakuen, I had a large number of faculty and staff for whom I needed to provide work. It was my obligation as headmaster of this corporate yet also familial institution to find new assignments for those no longer employed.

The most difficult faculty members to place were the small-animal veterinarians, since the large animal vets found new positions at nearby zoos. I approached this problem by asking the small-animal veterinarians to open a new pet hospital; however, they refused because of certain territorial agreements they had with the regional veterinary association. A new small-animal hospital in the area would take business away from existing ones—and there is an unwritten code among the veterinarians against doing this.

The next step was to ask the veterinarians about their fields of specialization. Two said they had a special technique to hatch chicken eggs. So the vets began planning our new chicken business. They were bright and ambitious; they knew a lot about genetics and how to breed the best chickens for eggs and others for meat. They suggested we buy a few American chickens to breed, because they were better suited genetically for egg production than native chickens of Japan. Although buying American birds and shipping them to Japan might sound like an expensive way of doing things, the overall costs in maintaining the chickens were much lower because of their genetic differences. Our goal had been to find or create a breed with the best feed-to-chicken ratio for the egg layers—and we were able to meet that goal by using the newly acquired American chickens.

Meanwhile, I asked my brother Yasuo, who had recently graduated from Keio at that time, about his future plans. He was unhappy at the ball-bearing manufacturing company where he had been working; after two or three years, he learned that the business wasn't his cup of tea. It was during this time that I became involved with an organization called the Young Presidents' Organization (YPO). This group gave me an opportunity to meet people from all corners of the business world. It was through YPO that I'd met the president of the discount supermarket Akafudadou (meaning "Red Tag House," or "Discount Warehouse"). I asked him to take Yasuo in for a couple of years so he could learn about the food and grocery business. After his short tenure at Akafudadou, I had Yasuo fly to the United States to study chicken farming for a couple of years so that he could eventually take my place as head of the newly formed chicken business. Yasuo agreed.

The veterinarians began planning the new chicken business. They were bright and ambitious doctors who knew a lot about genetics and how to breed the layer bird; however, they didn't know what to do afterward. And we had to find the best feed supplier for our chickens. We started selling chicks to the farmers but almost immediately found that the sales to the farmers were very inconsistent. Their requests might range from 10,000 to 50,000 birds, but at other times they might not want any chicks at all. The farmers' needs were highly unpredictable. To keep up with demand when it was there, we would continue to incubate eggs; yet more often than not we would have a number of extra birds that did not sell. We were forced to build chicken coops to raise these leftover chickens, a measure that only acted as a band-aid to the problem. The inconsistency of demand led us eventually to stop selling to farmers; we also decided to raise the chickens ourselves. Fortunately, I was able to engineer a merger with a supermarket chain to whom we could sell all our eggs. During the course of making a merger and building Jusco, I started talking with two other chains—Hotei-ya and Nishikawa-ya—about selling clothing to build a nationwide chain store. After a year and a half of intensive discussion with both companies, Takihyo agreed to create a new chain store that I christened Uny. The original thinking was that Hotei-ya and Nishikawa-ya and part of Takihyo would join together, thus creating a national chain store. However, some conflicts of interest arose and the merger could not be entirely completed. Regardless, Takihyo sent a mass of employees to help the restructuring of the companies and formation of the new management structure.

Although one egg—or dress or necktie—may not differ too much from another, you gain an unprecedented advantage in selling your product, whatever it may be, when you have a stronger relationship with a buyer. From the start, I knew the people that would become Uny customers and employees; they trusted me. Consequently, asking them to buy my products—whether it was food or clothing— was much easier. If competition arose between my company and another—and we both offered the same product—the people I knew would of course pick me and my relationship with them over the other unknown company. This was the basis upon which I started Taki Foods. After Yasuo's time of study in the United States, I relinquished my post to him. Unlike his experience in the ball-bearing business, Yasuo found a passion in the food services industry. He has grown the company to become one of the biggest chicken meat and egg sellers in the Nagoya area. Uny also has grown proportionately since the merger.

Although they may seem to have come out of left field, the solutions I found for Taki Gakuen came from the veterinarians and the resources to which I had access as president of Takihyo. Perhaps one of the most important lessons I learned in my first 10 years as Takihyo's president is that you must utilize all of your resources for the best results in order to solve a problem. You have to ask simple questions, regardless of how complex the answers to those questions might be.

The solutions I found for the Taki School did not arrive from an aha! moment or a monumental epiphany. I simply conducted basic research on how Taki Gakuen could fill the gaps among other neighboring schools. I understood my competition and retaliated with a hiring initiative promoting increased salaries for teachers. Others doubted my methods, but my plan yielded the desired results. My process could be described by combining two well-known sayings: there may be a hundred ways to skin the cat, but with a little preparation mountains become molehills. Taki Gakuen became a success in a matter of years rather than decades. Asking the simple questions—"What do I want to accomplish?" and "How can I help the consumer choose *us*?"—brought us the desired results. Although it might seem overly simplified, this theoretical framework grounds the way I break down complex problems into manageable-sized chunks. Today, Taki Gakuen remains one of the best K-12 private schools in Japan, and I am proud to have reified my grandfather's dream. After one of my other brothers, Katsuo, graduated from Keio University, I asked him to take care of the school, and he has done a wonderful job in its management.

Asking the Simple Questions

I have been advising managers across the world for more than 60 years, and I have never met someone as capable as Tomio Taki is of handling so many different problems simultaneously. What he calls "asking the simple questions" understates Taki's tremendous ability to be an effective manager and successful leader.

Although you will find many topics and questions to ponder throughout this book, there is really one underlying message at the core of everything Tomio does: his curiosity. My mother always said, "Strive not to be interesting, but to be curious. If you are curious, you will be interesting." It's been said that the late Nobel Laureate economist Milton Friedman never got off a plane without knowing the life story of the person seated beside him. His curiosity extended well beyond economics; Friedman wanted to find out what makes people tick. He wanted to see the bigger picture.

This openness to new situations is critical to managing any venture, as problems are inevitable. Keeping cool and calm gives a manager the room to be creative in devising an approach to problem solving. Asking the simple questions makes understanding a problem that much easier. Simple questions offer simple answers—and as Tomio argues, any problem can be solved with a strong foundation. Tomio's questioning helps him keep everything in perspective. He has never, no matter how profound the setback—and he has had his fair share—lost his capacity to wonder. Tomio cultivates his curiosity every moment. His example shows the power of curiosity to shape your life for the better.

Mortimer R. Feinberg, PhD

Wrap Up Japan

Respice, Adspice, Prospice[1]

---

[1]This Latin phrase means "a look at the past, at the present, and into the future."

The first part of this book focuses on my life in Japan from my early childhood until the late 1970s. In this concluding section I will explore my outlook on my native country's past, present, and future from a macro perspective. The lessons I learned over the course of my life demand a brief examination of what I believe to be a failing country. Inserting some insight into Japanese current affairs in light of my multinational experiences may add nuance to the histories I have included thus far: an examination of the past, present, and future prospects of Japan.

War was the absolute focus of attention in Japan in the earlier part of the twentieth century—war against the Chinese, Koreans, Russians, and later the Allied powers. Manufacturing, education, politics, and every other arena were geared toward winning the war. Before Japan threw up the white flag after Truman dropped the atom bomb on Hiroshima and Nagasaki, most of the important industrial, political, and commercial cities were bombed—and the infrastructure supporting the Japanese industrial machine was devastated.

Resources were scarce after the war, and the country was dirt poor. With little food and no money, many middle-class people were without water or electricity. The Japanese nation was brought to its knees and forced to live in very inadequate conditions. However, after all of the destruction on both sides, the Japanese nation had to stand and be counted as a part of the bigger picture. In the embrace of defeat, the government needed to step in to offer liquidity to the commercial markets. Entrepreneurs and business owners negotiated with banks in hopes of securing debt to start anew.

In May 1949, the Japanese state responded with the establishment of *Tsusho-sangyo-sho,*[2] known in Euro-America as the Ministry of

---

[2]通商産業省.

International Trade and Industry (MITI). This agency rose to become a dominant player until its dissolution a decade ago. Although this agency did so much, its primary concern had been to rebuild and to strategize an economic recovery for Japan. Without going into too much detail, I'll just say that MITI accomplished its aims first within the sector of light industry. Then MITI guided people toward the manufacture of light machinery and tools, and later toward heavy machinery, chemical, petrochemical, semiconductor businesses, and so on. The later wars in Korea and Vietnam also played a key role in the growth of heavy machinery and the auto trade in Japan. The United States began to use Japan as a base for the production of vehicles and other large machinery to help fight these wars. In turn, Japan received massive infusions of capital to capture their share of the defense and automotive markets.

However, prior to the inception of MITI, the shortage of capital led most Japanese companies to struggle. The government, the central bank, and the smaller regional banks had to work closely with the industries to help develop products at various stages. At that time, the Japanese population was very small in comparison to today— around 40 million. Therefore, domestic consumption alone could not justify a home-grown market. Japan had to depend on the success of its export businesses. A lack of significant natural resources in Japan further reinforced the necessity of successful export. Educational curricula were revised to nurture technicians, engineers, and scientists in an attempt to spawn innovation. However, after the war, the Japanese nation did not have sufficient industrial capacity and Japan was forced to enter the markets as a mimic of the West. The new mantra had been to buy a product overseas, knock it off, and add a little twist that might make it more desirable. Taking such cues from abroad, the domestic Japanese economy thrived and slowly gained a strong presence in international markets.

However, there was already a lot of competition in Japan—and the only way the country could grow would be to undercut current market prices. In addition, other than merely being less expensive, the Japanese added something intrinsically Japanese to its exports. Much like the incorporation of the Chinese character system as a foundation to the language with a native script, the Japanese culture influenced a mimicry and self-insertion in these products. In other words, the Japanese worldview had been to support and sustain an export economy; thus, the products manufactured needed to be both cheaper and in some way better than earlier versions and/or the competition's versions. In some cases, "better" meant more suited to the perceived Japanese consumer. This was the line of thought that led to the Sonys and Toyotas of today.

The automobile industry had a terrific break during the Korean and Vietnam Wars. After wartime, the factories had already been tooled to make all different kinds of vehicles. The majority of cars in Japan at the time had been imported from the United States. There was a large American military presence in Japan, prompting citizens to favor American-brand cars. However, these cars were suited for a particular kind of driving on long, flat roads; they were automobiles for which the Japanese cities and countryside proved less than accommodating. The narrow Japanese roads with tight corners and bumps were littered with potholes, causing cars to get nicked frequently and forcing drivers to proceed with caution.

The Japanese automakers responded to American innovation. Because of the conditions, they concentrated on manufacturing small, durable cars to navigate the treacherous roads and narrow streets safely. There were also economic incentives for these kinds of vehicles in Japan. The cost of oil went through the roof during the oil crisis of the early 1970s—causing automakers to set out to design the smallest car possible. The oil crisis of 1972 put the spotlight on Japanese cars. However, engineers did not account for the fact that Japanese-made cars would also be driven in other countries. Although these automobiles fared well in Japan, a reputation for their unreliability arose outside of the country. The engineers didn't stop to think that if the cars were driven on long highways, such as those in the United States, they might overheat and just stop. After many field tests, these fuel-efficient vehicles garnered more attention, and necessary improvements were made. The initial adjustments in automobile design suited a Japanese driver, but the engineers eventually learned to accommodate a much larger audience. This is why Toyota dominates today.

Playing catch-up for Japan worked very well for about 50 years. However, this rapid growth had to come to an end at some point. Japan established itself as a major exporter in an incredibly short period of time. It had been easy for Japanese industries to copy others' ideas and then make improvements upon them. Resting on the laurels of the West allowed Japan to coast its way to capitalist prosperity; however, there was stagnation once Japan caught up to the rest of the Western world. Much like most Western nations, the Japanese built upon previous generations—standing on the shoulders of others. This new precipice of economic stability required that the country devise a road map for the future—otherwise, further inactivity would ensue. And for the past 30 years, Japan has unfortunately struggled.

The Japanese population was growing until the last couple of decades. Perhaps this is an indicator of a developed nation: young Japanese men and women don't marry as much, and if they do, they average only one child per couple. Japanese people now want to relax and enjoy their lives. There is a catch-22, however, as slowing reproduction rates will more than halve the nation's population. The world's third largest economy may self-implode as a result of having fewer people and, consequently, less spending—both domestically and abroad. The Far East—and perhaps the entire world—relies on heavy Japanese consumption to sustain many of its industries.

This decreasing population affects every aspect of life, ranging from pension plans and health insurance to consumer businesses and real estate. The exponential rate of decline in population may result in a population of 70 million by 2060 from an already decreased number of 120 million today. Exacerbating matters will also be the ratio of elderly to young. Japan has only 1 million births a year at this time—a number that is sadly still decreasing. Some basic mathematics in combinations and permutations tells us that the Japanese population may shrink to 580 people in the year 2300 if nothing changes. In 2200, the Japanese will be added to the endangered species list. The probability that Japan will be a nation of 580 by 2300 is low but the country will halve without any significant changes in immigration policy in our lifetime. If the demographics continue to move in the same direction, this is what would happen but most likely policies will change.

Applying this logic to the retirement savings system, one person eligible to receive the government pension currently is supported by four working citizens. By 2060 the ratio could be one to one. Similar to the American Social Security system, the decline of which has been much discussed, Japan's pension system is not currently sustainable. Health insurance plans are supported by young and healthier workers as well, and those who seek medical assistance from the government tend to be elderly. When the ratio of the elderly to the young becomes too high, the current health care system will simply stop working—there will not be enough people paying into the system to support it.

Adding insult to injury, Japan's once ravenous consumer culture also has been stunted. I am not optimistic about Japanese retail markets; although retail stores are presently geared to cater to 120 million people, the current economic conditions have left mountains of inventory on the shelves with more price-conscious consumers. Overstock is then sold at whatever price consumers will pay. These massive discounts have started a microcosm of the deflationary environment in Japan. Consumers only begin to show interest once the big stores dump their inventory. In order to combat these kinds of problems, I believe that retail and office spaces should halve their sizes.

No matter one's social circles or place in the economic hierarchy, everyone in Japan will be negatively impacted by this dramatic transformation. Japan must stabilize the population by encouraging people to have more children or encourage immigration immediately. The latter has already begun to bring changes to the once homogeneous society. As with any change, many people simply don't like it. In fact, many fear that these kinds of changes may cripple politicians' campaigns. But without imported labor forces, Kansai Airport would never have been built, farmers could get no help, nursing homes would have no nurses, and garbage would be left on the streets. The average federal or municipal tax revenues have decreased, resulting in the country, municipalities, cities, towns, and villages finding themselves in terrible financial situations with no light at the end of the tunnel. The only hope is for the success of business to contribute to the country's infrastructure and economic growth.

The only way to increase profitability if domestic consumption shrinks is to sell products and services overseas and include other countries' populations in the market. The age-old requirement that Japanese companies keep employees has been rendered obsolete by international markets. More dynamic and flexible approaches to employment are necessary to compete. When Japan is the only nation to support lifetime employment, public companies become so-called value traps to foreign investors, and future growth can be stunted by obsolete divisions. This not only limits the amount of public equity available to the companies but also reinforces the market's perception of the potential value that could be unlocked within the company if such divisions were to be excised.

Most of these problems have arisen as a result of good intentions with poor execution. The Japanese political machine suffers from a kind of autoimmunity. The first architects of modern Japanese government had great vision. In the 1860s, the Meiji Revolution in Japan brought the brightest minds together to form a mix-and-match combination of various Western modern political systems, the structure of which has remained largely unchanged despite regime changes and the World Wars. However, this government is failing itself.

Modeled after the British, French, and American systems, Japan's government has the Emperor as figurehead with a Diet legislative arm supported by an executive branch headed by a Prime Minister; the executive and legislative branches provide the glue that holds the government together. There are also judiciary and police branches. In the United States' Federalist Papers, Alexander Hamilton, James Madison, and John Jay forged older ideas into a new, cohesive mix— one of their key innovations was the separation of branches of government to offer a novel system of checks and balances. Although Japan has these separate arms, there are almost no checks and balances between them. Perhaps the communitarian nature of the Japanese culture has skipped checks and balances, but at the end of the day, far too much fear of change exists. The US system is certainly not flawless, but there is and always has been contention among the House, the Senate, and the president. Recent financial reform and health care bills speak to this.

What makes matters worse is that many Japanese politicians have little knowledge of law. Instead, many come from good families that have previously been in politics; as a result, they believe that they and their offspring are fit to remain in the game. Much like the British system, the Prime Minister (PM) is elected from the house members of the majority party; he is not elected by the public. The PM appoints ministers according to seniority order, not because they have experience or special knowledge in a certain discipline. These appointees may have zero knowledge of what they are getting into. Consequently, minister appointees have to listen to or depend on their cabinet of ministers to tell them what to say and do. Under this system, the advisors of the ministry are the ones who end up proposing new laws. The PM then has the power to dictate terms to the Diet and pass the laws.

I believe that the executive branch should administer the law in the most efficient way possible to avoid confusion and increase solidarity. Members of his cabinet should not propose new laws; that is the supposed duty of the representatives. The current administration wants to change this so that all the ministers are able to propose new laws—something that seems ludicrous to me, considering how few of them have any legal experience. Chaos, in turn, has ensued, because it should be the Diet primarily proposing new laws and the executive arm administering them. I cannot say precisely how this system could be fixed, as it is outside of my area of expertise. However, it needs to be addressed; Japan needs new regulations—and much less confusion—for changing times.

The current world economic situation has forced Japanese businesses to move away from doing things the traditional Japanese way. If, for example, the general economy suffers in the United States, companies can trim the fat by firing unnecessary employees, closing divisions, and reducing expenses in an attempt to stay profitable. However, tradition has dictated that when someone is hired by a company in Japan, he or she is with that company for life. People interview for positions in the United States, letting their future employers know what they can and cannot do. In Japan kids fresh out of college have no experience and have never been exposed to business. They are hired and trained by a company for life. This is another reason why the Japanese economy has yet to recover: these companies shoulder the costs of unnecessary employees.

In a way, the Japanese nation is very wasteful. Even if a company does finally fire an employee, the employee may look only for another white collar, nine-to-five job, with all holidays respected. Employees want two weeks of vacation, and if they don't get it, their savings will allow them to hold out longer. However, their personal consumption drops as a result; there are articles in every major newspaper about the loss of the Japanese consumer in the international markets. Job seekers are selective even when unemployment is high. There is a tremendous shortage of employees in certain areas—nursing, trash collectors—even though salaries are relatively high and benefits are good.

Up until three decades ago, businesses were run by entrepreneurs or traditional conglomerate families. Even for companies like Toyota and Sony, the original founders, owners, or managers continue to remain very much involved in executive management. They are also involved in an economic group called the *Nippon Keizaidantairengoukai*,[3] or Japanese Business Federation, and have some influence over the country's economic policy. But for many companies today, their top executives are hired help; they stay in the position for a couple of years and then leave for a comfortable retirement. These short-term executives are not looking for a challenge. They try to pass their term safely and collect their payout. As I mentioned earlier, Japan has no natural resources. The only resource is its people.

Educating the nation is critical. To be hired by a large company, a student has to graduate from a top Japanese university. Alumni networks also play a large role in placement. Parents are therefore hesitant to send their children overseas to study because this networked structure is what will help them find jobs after they graduate. This system has hurt Japan's children more than helped them. Very few Japanese travel overseas, live in various countries, learn to speak other languages fluently, and see how other cultures function. It should be a top priority in the global world in which we live today for students to expand their knowledge outside of Japan—particularly because Japan's demographic and economic base has been shaken.

Another example testifying to this need for increased foreign exposure is the Japanese real estate bubble of the 1980s. Japanese companies were buying American real estate in excess—from Pebble Beach to Radio City Music Hall. At one point, it seemed that Japanese companies owned all of New York. However, these companies didn't enter US markets at the right time; also, the Japanese business executives had limited understanding of property values in other countries. There is a very limited amount of real estate in Japan, and demand has exceeded supply until recently; thus, all Japanese real estate purchasers assumed that real estate would be a guaranteed moneymaker abroad as it was at home. But overseas real estate is different; if the property isn't utilized, it doesn't produce profit and the price decreases. Just recently, we've seen the mortgage meltdown cripple the New York City real

---

[3] 日本経済団体連合会.

estate market, depressing prices by about 30 percent. Unlike in Japan, New Yorkers have nearby options for alternative locations to run their businesses. In fact, many international companies' headquarters are no longer in Manhattan, but in nearby New Jersey, Westchester County, and Connecticut. This migration out of the cities is a recent development in the United States.

Another massive stumbling block is the refusal to learn the culture behind the languages foreign to the Japanese. Even if a Japanese company buys an overseas establishment and sends a representative to that acquired company, the representative doesn't understand how to communicate with the local people. As a result, without any real exposure to the outside, it is almost impossible for a Japanese person to run any business outside of Japan, except into the ground.

Many companies acquired by Japanese companies have failed. Japanese management has a tendency to send a person to do a job for which he or she is not fit. Not trusting local management has been Japan's Achilles' heel. Japan is a very homogenous country; if you look around, you notice that everyone is Japanese. If you look around in the United States, on the other hand, you see people from everywhere. So whereas Americans basically know how to manage people who come from various countries and cultures, the Japanese have not had those opportunities or experiences. This leads to the potential for massive miscommunication, which can destroy any chance of managing multilingual—let alone multicultural—business societies.

Having said all of this, my thoughts about the necessary improvements in Japan are to establish strong leadership, domestically and internationally. Japan is a small country without a military, so to speak. How can it exist in the world? We have to consider five different branches, economically speaking:

1. **Trade**—both export and import
2. **Capital investment**—domestic and international
3. **Stock**—purchasing and selling (investments inclusive of currency)
4. **Service**—transportation, communication, etc.
5. **Intellectual property**—patents, inventions, brands, software, etc.

Leadership has to put emphasis on one of these fields. We can foresee a trade deficit because it is very costly to manufacture in Japan, so most manufacturing is now subcontracted overseas. A primary concern should be to focus on capital improvement—welcoming investment from overseas into Japan to strengthen the financial sector, introduce new technologies, and work together with Japanese methods of innovation. Finally, a major problem in Japan today is taxation. I would propose getting rid of taxes, except for real estate taxes, which would contribute to domestic revenue for local municipalities. We have been putting a tremendous amount of energy toward trying *not* to pay taxes. The amount of money and time that each individual and corporation spends on this is astonishing. We would be much better off if we could eliminate these. Money transferred or deposited into a bank or institutional account should have 2 percent automatically deducted to cover all taxes. This would reduce both individual companies' and the government's costs across the board in terms of salaries, expenses, and so on. Basically, most people who work at the tax office are looking for errors in order to collect more tax: a very expensive and time-consuming system. Therefore, eliminating the need for such intensive auditing would offer an incredible boost to everyone's bottom line.

PART 2

United States

My first decade as a manager had been incredibly rewarding in both corporate and personal spheres. The Stacy Ames launch—along with a host of smaller projects tied to the Bobbie Brooks fashion house—not only changed how Takihyo did business but also revolutionized women's fashion in Japan. Never before had a large company taken such a leap of faith into an unknown territory with such positive results. There's a saying in Japan: "The nail that sticks up gets hammered down." In other words, it's better to stay with what's been done in the past, and don't try anything new. However, our experience with the Stacy Ames brand disputed this axiom; the brand's newness stuck out and in the process brought legitimacy to manufacturing and wholesaling Western-style women's wear in Japan.

Of course, fashion had been changing all over Japan. The climate had been ripe for such a transformation, but no one, including me, foresaw the strength of demand for Western-style women's wear. Takihyo's initiatives led to dresses flying off the racks in weeks.

In addition to offering Western-style clothing in Japan, completing the Marunouchi Building—Nagoya's first high-rise—under budget and ahead of schedule with the Takenaka Construction Company was a major accomplishment. There were high-rises in Japan, of course, but none in Nagoya. The other construction companies building high-rises in Japan were based out of the three major cities—Osaka, Tokyo, and Kyoto. I viewed the Marunouchi Building as an investment for both Takihyo and for the city: I was betting on Nagoya's imminent vertical climb in the decades to come.

The ventures furnishing the building were also quite successful—particularly Takihyo's joint venture with the US company Steelcase to manufacture the building's modular office furniture in the Far East. Being able to transform a rigid office space into one that can be anything from a showroom to a conference room with little physical effort redefined what *office space* meant for our company. If we needed a runway at the last minute, we could have one without too much of a fuss. This change dramatically boosted sales, thus increasing our exposure and making it much easier to market our products. The flexibility of our space increased productivity and the salability of our goods.

The newly established Chu-Bu Distribution Center added to the excitement. Our offices became our own. We no longer shared space with inventory, which increased productivity in the office: administrators, directors, and managers could focus on their allotted tasks rather than shipping and receiving. Housing the inventory in a new place also proved more economical per square meter and increased the ease of tracking parcels thanks to our enhanced shipping and receiving organization. I came up with this idea from some of my travels to the United States when I noticed how American offices functioned. I preferred this environment to the traditional Japanese methods to which I was accustomed. The distribution center helped channel our inventory from the manufacturing plants to the end consumer faster and more effectively. Aside from the new distribution process, which I discussed in an earlier chapter, Takihyo was also forging new relationships with mom-and-pop clothing stores.

Although most of Takihyo's goods were distributed to our Jusco and Uny chain stores, our business also focused on wholesaling garment products and textiles. I wanted Takihyo to diversify and expand its distribution channels beyond the big chain stores to smaller stores. Under my guidance, Takihyo invested in a few small companies to grow existing distribution channels. Tokyo Style was one company with which I helped establish a working relationship. We negotiated terms of credit with Tokyo Style in exchange for information about what fabrics and items moved in the market. This credit line allowed Tokyo Style to expand its market share but also gave us the information we needed at the consumer level. For instance, if there were 100 orders for a particular garment in a certain month, but Tokyo Style did not have capital for materials, Takihyo would offer credit to fulfill the order. Takihyo advanced textiles and garments to satisfy the end consumer's needs through manufacturers with which we had established good relationships. With little risk on our part, Takihyo helped Tokyo Style grow into the large company it is today. By the late 1960s, Takihyo was in the best shape it had been in since its inception.

The revolutions, discoveries, and innovations responsible for birthing cultures and countercultures across the globe marked the feel of the 1960s. From the new styles in popular music to the foundations of modern civil rights, the decade became synonymous with change. Although my life represents only a point in this mass movement to difference, the growth of my family's company and school ushered in a new era of protocols and conventions for Japanese fashion. There could not have been a more exciting historical period to be a Japanese businessman in the textile and garment industries.

On the other hand, the changes of the 1970s in Japan revolved around international diplomacy and subsequent transformations in economic and political policies. Japan is geographically a very small country. Although the country's population had been growing for quite some time before the 1970s, more goods were being manufactured than consumed—and most ended up in the export market. From 1944 until 1971, the Bretton Woods system was in place to guide financial and commercial relations across international lines. This system touted a gold exchange standard, to which all internationally trading countries adhered: gold acted as currency for international trade. After MacArthur's occupation of Japan during the Korean and Vietnamese Wars, the United States used Japan not only as a base for military operations but also for the manufacturing of arms and vehicles. These operations gave Japan an economic jump on China and Korea, and they also further fortified Japan's relations with the United States. Consequently, the Japanese people and government felt comfortable economically even though the nation was still politically and militarily subject to US power.

Within the last couple of years of his first term as US president, Richard Nixon shook the world twofold—the so-called Nixon shocks of 1971 and 1972. These shocks impacted the globe, but the potential consequences for Japan were particularly devastating. The first Nixon shock was the eradication of the Bretton Woods system. The United States had spent most of its gold during the Korean and Vietnamese Wars, not to mention the costs of the preceding First and Second World Wars. Nixon saw a potential shift in power and loss of economic prowess if he kept the Bretton Woods Accord in place. Although Japan (and many other exporting nations) had been piling up gold, the United States and its allies had nearly depleted their resources. Lyndon Johnson's economic and political policies and Great Society programs decimated American finances; Nixon yearned to reinvigorate the American economy to guarantee future American economic strength.

In a way, the Nixon shocks solidified America's relationship with Japan. After the Second World War, the American occupation effectively rewrote the Japanese constitution. In the ninth article, Japan is forbidden to have a standing army and to wage war against another nation. Under the Treaty of Mutual Cooperation and Security signed after the occupation in 1960, the United States became an ally to a state without a standing army. In short, after the occupation, the United States has been required to protect Japan, as attacking Japanese soil is equivalent to attacking the United States Consequently, keeping America wealthy, or at least balancing the budget, would serve to protect Japanese interests. On the other hand, the Japanese were upset because all of the gold collected was now being traded on a commodity market unrelated to the dollar—a move that potentially threatened Japan's financial stability. Exporting countries like Japan were hurt and surprised by such a radical shift in economic policy—what were they supposed to do with stockpiles of gold with no monetary value?! The outcome, as we can see today, was not as grim as predicted at the time. However, the first Nixon shock set a tone for change that the Japanese people were not ready for.

Nixon's second shock was to open a window for trade with China the following year. Not that this was really such a surprising political maneuver, although Nixon had kept all premeditation secret until after the talks. His clandestine politics conjured in the Japanese feelings of betrayal: they worried that the United States wanted to open trade with a former Japanese enemy without the new Japanese leadership finding out. At the end of the day, however, Nixon's changes were brilliant. Everyone benefited, including the Japanese.

These two events led to questions about the value of the US dollar and the force that US politics wields to manipulate international economies. The United States pushed the Japanese to rethink terms and guidelines for cooperation and reconciliation with previous enemies, thereby planting the seeds to spur future growth.

After the Yom Kippur War, Egypt, Syria, and the Arab members of OPEC put an oil embargo temporarily on the United States for sending $2.2 billion in emergency aid to Israel. This embargo led to the oil crisis, or Oil Shock of 1973—which deeply impacted the Japanese economy. Since 1945, Japan had depended on American markets and demands. The Korean and Vietnamese Wars provided Japanese industry room for growth and steady state-sponsored business manufacturing tanks, cars, airplanes, helicopters—you name it—for the US military. The first Oil Shock brought Japanese consumer spending to a standstill. Much like what occurred during the 2008–2009 recession, the Japanese people no longer sought after luxury or high-end goods. In terms of fashion, men and women wore the same clothes year after year, rather than replenishing according to the season's trends.

These events played a pivotal role in Takihyo's history in the 1970s. We had become accustomed to increased consumer spending from the decade before, and so we did not foresee such a dramatic shift. This break from the past annihilated distribution channels and forced us to shut down a number of once-lucrative divisions, including the Steelcase joint venture and the carpet-manufacturing business. In the following chapter, I will discuss how these historical events had a detrimental effect on both my corporate and personal life.

CHAPTER 7

The Break from Culture

A new era had emerged—one in which Takihyo's fiscal strength came into question. The 1970s demonstrated the susceptibility of all companies—no matter how high the quality of the product, the management, or the institution—to macroeconomic stress. The demand for dresses that had previously flown off the shelves evaporated. Once-profitable subdivisions fell from well into the black to deep into the red. For the first time since my appointment as the chief executive, Takihyo held rather than distributed warehouses of inventory. We were bleeding; we needed relief. Many feared that the Nixon shocks and the oil and energy crises would bury Takihyo.

Because textile-and-garment manufacturing and wholesaling comprised the bulk of Takihyo's revenue stream, we held a lot of inventory. In healthy markets, demand within distribution channels dictates the flow of goods: some to regional chain stores like Uny and Jusco, and others to regional wholesalers. In normal markets, goods are in constant flow; however, the slump in consumer demand during the early 1970s forecasted a different—and difficult—road ahead.

The upside to manufacturing and wholesaling is the elimination of the middleman. We create and distribute, so there are no agent or licensing fees for sales. Instead of introducing a third party, we would reap the benefits of higher profit margins by utilizing in-house wholesaling after production; instead of one area in which we could profit, there were now two. In other words, if a textile manufacturer can make 15 cents on every dollar and a wholesaler can make the same margin of profit, the one who can do the job of *both* manufacturer and wholesaler winds up not with 30 cents on the dollar, but a little more.

The downside, however, is just as significant. Typically, Takihyo manufactures in accordance with demand. Manufacturing and wholesaling entails doing both in tandem and requires that planning be done farther in advance than would be required when doing either one or the other of the processes alone. Therefore, combining the two creates a higher gain with more risk because change slows with each added element.

Unfortunately, there was no way we could have predicted the oil crises of the 1970s or Nixon's politics. The first crisis occurred after a season of textiles and garments had neared completion. With hundreds of distribution channels and nearly as many brands, stopping the manufacturing process was not an option. We had nowhere to place inventory when our primary distribution channels dried up.

Speculation[1] dictates how and what Takihyo manufactures. Before the slump in demand, we made textiles, then garments, months in advance. When the first oil crisis hit, we kept a season's worth of clothing that normally went to hundreds of stores. Then the political and economic crises left us naked. No one would consider taking inventory off our hands, because no one wanted the risk of carrying any extra—they worried about inventory and wages eating up capital. The nation stopped in its tracks, and that paralysis shook Takihyo; we were left with approximately $40 million of extra inventory.

---

[1]Here I use the term *speculation* as Benjamin Graham uses it in *The Intelligent Investor,* edited by Jason Zweig (New York: Harper Collins, 2003). According to Graham, a speculative position is one made by using a lesser calculus, which makes it riskier than an investment that retains value or grows in value slowly and steadily.

The way I dealt with this problem had a lot to do with the context of Japanese business culture in which I was working. Hierarchic structure rules the work environment in Japan. Although the highest executives have the most power, they tend to offer middle-level management most of the opportunity "to make or break" themselves within the company. Upper management takes the brunt for subordinates' mistakes, but the companies' officers tend to make general, sweeping suggestions rather than giving absolute directives. This way of thinking allows up-and-coming managers the room to develop within the corporate structure.

However, there's a catch. As middle managers may make all the calls, there is a system to which traditional Japanese management adheres called *ringi* or *ringisho*.[2] In most circumstances, *ringisho* is nothing more than a mere formality: a system in which employees submit suggestions to management in the form of a circular letter that touches colleagues' desks until it reaches superiors. These letters or notes are passed every day and require stamps with the *kanji*[3] of colleagues' surnames to approve all the different ideas. If a friend wants to propose a suggestion, favoritism can play a role in supporting the idea. Regardless of whether the suggestion pertains to trivial or substantive matters, the notes or letters reach the managing directors' desks for approval or rejection. In the case of rejection, executives offer the employee constructive criticism so that they can modify the letter or note to remove their suggestion before it is implemented. Although many cultures discourage the practice of employees' criticizing superiors, it's welcomed in Japan.

The company is the most important element to employees and managers because it provides everything from health care to one's daily bread. Someone from the Western world would likely ask, "Why would a subordinate criticize an executive? Wouldn't that get him a one-way ticket to unemployment?" The answer is simply, "no." There are many assumptions that Westerners make when doing business in the Far East—especially executives who move there to manage people—and subordinate disenfranchisement is one of them.

---

[2] 稟議書.

[3] *Kanji* are Chinese characters that have been assimilated into the Japanese written language. The stamps used are called "Hanko."

The reason for this is that employees have very strong job security in Japan. In many companies, especially in the 1970s, employees do not fear getting fired; however, they do care more about the company as a whole than about their direct superiors.[4]

Unlike in the United States, there are very few formal labor unions in Japan, and those that do exist remain within specific industries such as electronics or steel and iron manufacturing. On the other hand, most Japanese companies have an employee base that functions as a union within the company. This model puts the company's health in the hands of employees. The company carries a reciprocal relationship of responsibility with its workers. Because the organization's future dictates the prospects of the employee's own future, Japanese employees do not try to run the company's well dry by asking for raises or payments in advance. Indeed, it benefits Japanese employees to keep the company's best interest at heart—because these organizations offer lifetime positions. If the company grows and does well, employees will see opportunity for upward mobility. If, on the other hand, a firm shrinks or goes bankrupt, the employee has no economic lifeline, no support, and definitely no guarantees.

In United States, however, American unions rule American industries; unions are plentiful and involved in nearly every industry. Regardless of how well or poorly a company that employs union workers performs, union leaders are only directly responsible to union members. Although this structure hurts businesses that have to work with the unions—and occasionally troubles nonunion workers—the American system offers benefits and hourly wages far greater than what normally would be offered for a comparable job in private industry. Also, it pretty much guarantees employment. From a macroeconomic perspective, higher union fees and related payroll expenses bring more consumers to the marketplace; however, from an entrepreneurial perspective, American unions increase start-up costs and delays while limiting the company's growth and capital cushions with these same expenses.

In terms of loyalty, the Japanese company structure puts the organization before the superior. Therefore, the corporate institution caters to

---

[4]Although these attitudes are slowly changing today, in more traditional companies employees' sense of responsibility and allegiance to the company still hold true.

and provides for the individual. This mentality liberates the employee from the fear of speaking out that is so prevalent in the West. In an American company, employees may fear their boss's rejection of an idea. People's motives are often hard to understand; a superior may consider the employee to be too self-serving and decide as a result that he or she doesn't merit employment. Because the Japanese company's best interest is in line with the employee's—and because the employee does not fear rejection in the same way—opinions on operation can spread like wildfire.

From another light, Japanese traditional corporate culture holds every member of the organization accountable. Everyone has a duty to chip in when handling issues ranging from client relations and product placement to marketing, merchandising, and advertising. The consequences of this kind of thinking extend far beyond this particular application. For example, when employees go on strike this mentality extends to subversive behaviors. The striking employees do not stop working. Instead, they wear armbands while working to display dissatisfaction with the company.

This example illustrates the culture's emphasis on humility and honor rather than proactive disengagement and picketing. The employee does no damage to the company itself, but instead attempts to inflict harm on the company's public image. However, if the company cannot meet the employee's expectations, the employee has two options: resign or concede. In many cases, the employees will concede and carry on a respectful relationship with superiors and subordinates. In other words, the Japanese company manifests a communitarian environment with a collective and self-critical approach to responsibility.

I discuss these elements of Japanese culture to illustrate how different everyday life is in Japan vis-à-vis life in Europe or America. The cultural undercurrents can inform how managers decide—whether for good or bad. At times, a manager has to look past culture to find solutions. Yet doing so can cause upheaval, especially at large and traditional companies like Takihyo. The circumstances of the times forced me to disregard those cultural undercurrents to shield Takihyo as well as I could from inevitable losses during the oil crises and Nixon shocks. This allowed me to distinguish between a nation's corporate culture and its corporate climate—a topic I will discuss in the following chapter.

On Responsibility and Culture

A wise sage observed that there are six phases to a project:

1. Enthusiasm
2. Disillusionment
3. Panic
4. Search for the guilty
5. Punishment of the innocent
6. Praise and honors for the nonparticipant

Let's use these parameters to analyze how American managers differ from their Japanese peers. The Western executive has a tendency—albeit not always, but on occasion—to strive to find a lower-level scapegoat. The Japanese, on the other hand, turn upward. They believe the top of the tree is always ultimately responsible. They believe that if a subordinate created an error that may have cost the company millions of lost revenues, the chief executive officer (CEO) is actually at fault—because he or she should have never put that person in a role where so much damage could be done. For example, if people suffer food poisoning in a Japanese restaurant, the head chef commits *hari-kari* (ritual suicide)—not the assistant bottle washer.

I heard the story of one particular CEO whose accountant requested that he start cutting salaries and bonuses during a significant financial downturn. He agreed, but said, "Let's first start with my direct reports. Then we will see if we need to go further down the food chain." This man took the approach of someone who ran a Japanese company: in a crisis, look up, not down. After all, as the great WWII commander General Joseph Stilwell said: "The higher a monkey climbs, the more his rear is exposed."

Mortimer R. Feinberg, PhD

CHAPTER 8

Outside Factors Wound Takihyo

The company netted about $100 million during the year of my success with the Stacy Ames brand. Our estimates reflected Takihyo's recent growth from licensing agreements with Bobbie Brooks, other various start-up divisions, and a general increase in revenue for the following year. We predicted a tremendous increase in sales in early 1973, so we invested about $20 million more into manufacturing and wholesaling overhead. Accordingly, we increased our output for the year. We bought more fabrics and raw materials to provide for what we saw as a growth in demand.

After the oil crisis of 1973, Japanese consumer demand was crippled. Simultaneously, the costs of our material and production commitments continued to grow—a devastating combination of factors. Japanese citizens were no longer buying carpeting and high-fashion items; traditional wood flooring was more economical than our mats, and a woman would wear an old dress a few more times, as long as it was carefully washed. Consumers considered most new goods to be extraneous, luxury expenses. People were more concerned with stocking up on necessities like soap, toilet paper, bottled water, and canned foods. The price of petrol products, including gas and oil, spiked with the announcement of the OPEC embargo in 1973; oil quadrupled to $12 per barrel by 1974. Because Takihyo used petrol products for a number of our fashion lines—such as polyesters and polypropylene in our carpeting division—we ran into trouble when the price of the materials spiked. We could no longer afford to buy materials to manufacture and distribute products to meet lackluster public demand. Carrying loss was not an option for us, particularly because of how quickly fashion changes from one season to the next.

We incurred massive operating losses during that year. Many of our clients weren't capable of receiving the goods we had previously contracted to provide for them. And because consumers were no longer buying, our wholesaling businesses suffered. Even if we were in contract with retailers, we couldn't give them product they couldn't sell. Not only would it be a poor marketing and public-relations decision on Takihyo's part, but retailers would just return the inventory anyway. After spending time with Takihyo's accounting department and directors, we calculated an approximate $40 million[1] loss—t aking into account all warehousing fees and inventory losses. However, this was just the number we put on the books; we estimated an increase of revenue at three to four times the incurred loss before the oil crisis. Before the change in the political climate, our figures projected steady—and quite strong—company growth.

Whenever I discuss this moment in Takihyo's history, people tend to ask me what I would have done differently. The answer to that question is simple: nothing. However rocky the political narrative had been since WWII, more happened to help the Japanese country and people than anything else. Although there were many horrifying atrocities of war, the Korean and Vietnamese conflicts brought sustained economic benefit to Japan. Without those wars, many companies—particularly heavy industry in Nagoya and other Japanese cities—would not have grown so quickly. Beginning with

---

[1]In 2010, the loss is the equivalent of $196,000,000.00 using the consumer price index as a benchmark. The CPI here is used because Takihyo caters to typical consumers and therefore the change in the cost of buying goods for most consumers offers the most accurate basis for difference in value over time. Statistics from "Measuring Worth" (www.measuringworth.com/index.html).

the Japanese surrender in 1945, the US and Allied forces have used Japan as a strategic military zone, including manufacturing everything from vehicles to communications devices. Although they were funded with US money for US use, this financial support also laid the infrastructure for Japan's future. These circumstances allowed Japan to industrialize faster than any other country in history. It took a mere 60 years for the nation to begin to benefit from becoming a home base for multiple wars.[2]

The wars increased earnings and spending per capita in Japan as well. The economic boost not only offered good-paying employment to the masses but provided inroads for industry to develop. Japan enjoyed exponential economic growth with great momentum ahead of it. Before the oil crisis, I saw no reason why production would slow for our company. The oil crisis was entirely unpredictable and left us without any means of preemptive action. Nevertheless, the corporate, social, and political climate changed.

I have also been asked, "Why couldn't you stop production and return materials as the retailers returned to you?" Simply put, it is essentially impossible to *stop* in the middle of production. Once the raw materials are purchased, they are sent directly to the textile mill, which then passes the fabrics along to the garment manufacturing plant. After the goods are made, they are sent to the distribution center—then off to retailers. This process is set into motion with the first step. Nothing can be recouped if garments are only half-completed.

I offer the following example to further clarify: half of the raw materials are finished textiles and ready for transportation for production, while the other half is still being processed; the first half is then distributed, putting the chain of production and distribution of the garment in motion. After completion, the first half is shipped to the distribution center to await the production of garments from the second half of finished materials to fulfill the order before mass distribution. Now, imagine that there were as many as seven or eight separate parts rather than two to manufacture one out of hundreds of garments.

---

[2]Although there are many texts to consult, perhaps the most exacting is John Dower's *Embracing Defeat: Japan in the Wake of World War II* (New York: W. W. Norton & Co., 2000).

What makes matters worse is the fact that inventory is not completely taken into account until it reaches the distribution center. Sometimes, there are delays in production; materials arrive late or only half an order is put to work at once. Output results are not always on a dime and can be either larger or smaller than expected. What further confused the accounting was that Takihyo did not manufacture everything it distributed, and did not distribute everything it manufactured. For example, we sometimes bought textiles to make garments because the manufacturing was different from what we could produce. We also wholesaled textiles and finished garments to other companies. The number of agreements we had for the amount of inventory we kept and sold needed a distribution center's tracking. However, by the time the products were counted and numbered, it was already too late to avoid the macroeconomic conditions. There was no way for Takihyo to avoid this loss.

Despite the rate at which the red ate up Takihyo's balance sheet, my only recourse was to step back and develop a managerial strategy to combat losses. I proposed that Takihyo's convalescence—recovering from the impacts of the oil crisis, Nixon shocks, and the energy crisis of 1979—was a three-step process. First and foremost, we had to close all unprofitable divisions; second, clear leftover inventory; and last, establish new lines of credit with a bank to cover losses and to continue profitable operations.

I wanted to stop the bleeding quickly and efficiently. Excising burdensome divisions meant no payroll, inventory, and overall operating expenses to pay; it would give us the breathing room Takihyo needed. There is a saying in Japan: "If you are going to climb a mountain, you want to have the least amount of weight on your back." Once the divisions were closed and we had a bridge loan in place, we could pay off debt and streamline to make Takihyo leaner and meaner.

I also wanted another way out if it turned out that we were in more trouble than we had initially thought. In retrospect, one of the most important lessons I have learned is that you need not one but two, three, four, or more ways to exit safely—for any venture. If all else fails, I always want there to be another plan to execute. This methodology provides multiple solutions for the complex problems of the future. Creating solutions *before* the problems arise is preemptive action; nothing else suffices. What many deem to be a sense of optimism, I see not as a confidence in execution but as comfort in risk-reward analysis. My worst-case scenario looked bright in the instance of Takihyo's $40 million loss in the 1970s: I always had the option to sell Nagoya's first high-rise building. The Marunouchi Building was not only built as an investment; selling it could be the key to escaping any possible future financial distress.

Because companies in Japan carry a social function closer to that of the Western concept of the family, I had an obligation to those in the closing divisions. It was my duty as the president and patriarch to look out for those who had so earnestly worked for the company, however long their tenure; this was especially true for those who were hired for a venture I started. They needed employment, but Takihyo could not afford to keep all of them—which was the case for most companies at the time. I had to call in favors from a number of friends in various industries. In the end, a combined effort from all levels of management helped us find placements for these individuals.

I also planned a potential revival for the closing divisions if and when the time was right. Because we had already invested time, energy, resources, and money into proper distribution channels and branding, the doors had already been opened for Takihyo to reintroduce that particular product to the market. In my view, closing a division opened doors for future business in the same field—especially since closing equates with the reallocation of current resources. This line of thinking, though, was all-expansive.

I sold any of the dead-weight inventory at whatever the market would take. Carrying inventory that won't sell is like saving cracked eggs; it only results in putrid smells and a mess in the kitchen. Many of the other managers tried to convince me to save products for a rosier economic climate. They seemed to forget how much it costs per square meter to store $40 million worth of inventory. I calculated that the overhead far exceeded the margins of profit, provided that the world economy would bounce back in a couple of years. The arguments other directors and board members made held no relevance to the times for me. It seemed cleaner to rid the company of any malignancies and strive forward in hopes for a brighter future, while still expecting less. At the end of the year, we brought in approximately $80 million—but lost $40 million in inventory and associated costs.

Takihyo had reached a point where it couldn't function without
some kind of financial help. I needed to look outside the company. As
I recounted earlier, I took a loan from a family-friend's bank—then
called The Tokai Bank, Ltd.—after my father died. I was now in a
situation nearly as dire and had very few other places to look for help.
I called Tokai again to ask for a loan to cover the company's losses.
Comparatively speaking, the size of our loan—$40 million—was the
equivalent of $220 million in today's dollars.[3] In other words, it was a
huge loan, and because we were a nearly 200-year-old company working with a publicly observed bank, media attention was inevitable.

The bank needed some time to figure things out and get back to
me. Tokai offered me the help I needed, but on the condition that the
bank would appoint an overseer to report on how Takihyo conducted
business. Tokai understandably wanted an insurance policy against the
massive loan. The financial trouble Takihyo faced seemed daunting
from the outsider's perspective. Taking such a large loan makes an unin-
formed spectator question management. The bank didn't want to take
any risks and I needed to convince them why Takihyo was not at risk.

Some people thought that I was driving the company—along
with the $40 million—into the ground. The bank wanted some way
to control any potential for loss and the bankruptcy protection that
could ensue. They arranged someone from an Osaka branch who
was about to retire to oversee the repayment of the loan to Tokai in
Nagoya. I didn't really have a choice; this individual would take an
executive role at the company.

As I mentioned before, although there are no real unions in Japan,
companies function as families. This makes it incredibly difficult to
fire staff, especially those who have served their entire tenure at one
company. In most cases, Japanese companies can only push people to
retire or to quit. The individual that Tokai Bank sent was an old executive who probably should have been fired but couldn't be, due to
the Japanese corporate system and the bylaws protecting employees.
This flaw in Japanese corporate structure led to a harried and slow
recovery for Takihyo after we took the loan. It also put tremendous
pressure on my personal life.

---

[3]See footnote 1.

My friend from Tokai Bank called me to tell me that someone named Mr. Ito was coming into Takihyo as an executive vice president. I knew nothing about who he was or what his history had been other than his relationship with the bank. I was fully aware of the possibility that this individual could be a bad employee. I figured that it was temporary anyway and that it wouldn't be too bad as long as he didn't interfere too much. Unfortunately, he was more involved than I expected him to be.

When the loan became public knowledge, the story was printed in the papers. A number of friends and colleagues from Osaka called me to warn me about Mr. Ito's character, but there was little I could do to reverse the decision at that point. Not only had the announcement been publicly made, Tokai had treated the situation as a *fait accompli*. I also knew that I couldn't worry too much; at the end of the day, my plans for Takihyo were quite optimistic despite our recent financial problems.

But I started to see my plan deteriorate after Mr. Ito's arrival, as he began reporting false information to the bank. I am unsure what his motive was in doing so; perhaps he wasn't really paying attention to the business, or perhaps he was misinformed. In any case, his relationships, with me and with the company's directors, were neither helpful nor productive.

Mr. Ito started talking to the media about elements of the business without my or anyone else's consent; he only offered information that was to the detriment of the company. At that point, Takihyo started to look like it was going under, as far as the public was concerned—despite the fact that we truly did have the assets to support our losses. Mr. Ito's refusal to dig deeper and give Takihyo an honest representation to the media—to whom he shouldn't have been talking without the company's consent anyway—and to Tokai Bank took nearly a decade to repair.

Making matters worse, the consequences of Mr. Ito's actions and Takihyo's subsequent, painfully slow rebound reverberated into my private life. My wife, the mother of my twin boys, saw only the press hounding us daily for news of the company's imminent failure. She had been raised in the traditional Japanese style; the embarrassment and loss of honor that she felt we would both experience was too much for her to bear. In 1978, she took her own life. I mourned her loss in the traditional Buddhist fashion: I shaved my head, and I temporarily broke contacts with the outside world. However, I wouldn't let Takihyo's losses and Mr. Ito's path of destruction destroy me too. My wife's death traumatized me; however, I was confident that there was still much left in store.

Leave-taking

It is very difficult to write—or read—about death with any degree of clinical objectivity. When someone we love dies, all of the mechanisms of leave-taking come into play with intensity unparalleled by any other experience. There is a universal tendency for people to deny loss in response to such a tragedy. When a loved one dies, survivors often cannot believe that the death has occurred, thus impelling certain psychic mechanisms to operate as if indeed it had not taken place. This is sometimes referred to as magical thinking. Although a number of misguided doctors sedate people suffering from acute grief, many physicians and psychologists are now alert to the dangers in this tendency. They realize that mourning is a critical therapeutic process.

When Tomio Taki's wife committed suicide, the world briefly stopped for the young, up-and-coming manager. He slowed down; for a short while, he disappeared. Tomio and I had met only a few years before at a number of Young Presidents' Organization universities,[4] and I met his wife Yoko as well; she was beautiful and reserved. A few months after her death, Tomio recounted to me that in the Buddhist tradition, he shaved his head in mourning for her. He took time from his duties and obligations as the leader of one of Japan's largest textile and garment businesses to gather his thoughts and cope with her death. He also had two boys in their teens in great need of his support.

[4]YPO terms the "university" as a place for young presidents to come together and learn with one another. These two- to three-day events are conferences.

Mariners know that when a typhoon strikes, the greatest danger is that the ship will *broach to*—come broadside to the waves. When this happens, the vessel no longer answers to the helm. The wind and sea take command and the ship is in deadly peril of sinking or capsizing. To try to run before the storm is to increase the danger; the only hope is to heave to and ride it out. *Heaving to* means slowing down the boat's forward motion to lessen the impact of the surrounding wake. Although huge waves wash over the decks and superstructure, the ship can survive. Somehow and in some way, Tomio understood that the best policy during the first moments of trauma was simply to ride it out. He distanced himself from the corporate world to heave to and let the waves break over himself. Such waves of pain were quite hard for him to handle, but instead of fleeing or self-medicating, Tomio confronted these pains by mourning.

A healthy psyche will repair the damaged or broken threads. The work of mourning is necessary to the process. But the mind needs emotional resiliency to do this. When we are constantly involved with other people and forced to think about other things, the work of mourning is deferred. Furthermore, our emotional resiliency—already low—is exhausted. The bereaved person who is distracted all day long will go through the work of mourning only in the late hours of night; F. Scott Fitzgerald's "dark night of the soul, when it is always three o'clock in the morning."

If Tomio had not taken the time on his own to suffer, mourn, and grieve for the loss of his wife, he would have never continued on his route to his successes in the mid-to-late 1980s. The 1970s brought Tomio his lowest of low periods, from the closing of many of Takihyo's divisions to his wife's suicide. However, the 1970s—as mentioned in the introduction to Part 2—were also a time of astronomical growth, a time during which Tomio planted the seeds for future growth far greater than anything previously anticipated. I believe this could be accomplished only because Tomio took the time to mourn.

(continued)

(continued)

Tomio gave himself time alone when he was hit by his wife's suicide. From a professional standpoint, he couldn't have reacted in a better way. He mourned; he let the process go forward. Sometimes people act as if there were a sliding scale of mourning: a year for the death of a husband or wife, 10 months for a parent, 8 months for a divorce, 6 months for a separation—down to 30 seconds for a pair of cuff links. But life doesn't work that way. The loss that seems trivial according to conventional standards may hit us harder than what is assumed by others to be a major blow. In other words, we must all take the time to heal in times of need—whether it's from a personal loss or a professional one—as Tomio did so appropriately.

Mortimer R. Feinberg, PhD

CHAPTER 9

Now, the Good

The 1970s were a time that challenged me more than any other period of my life. The personal tragedies I endured over the course of that decade tested my inventive capacity, wits, and confidence. Luckily, I was still young and my ambition remained. Furthermore, my personal experiences kept me intact in the face of defeat. Watching the Second World War unravel behind the convoluted lens of my early youth while living in an evacuation camp had given me the strength to carry on. Even in the uncertain economic climate of the 1970s, I laid the foundations for Takihyo's future—not only in Japan but also abroad. Some of my initiatives that began in the midst of the political and economic turmoil of the early Nixon era fashioned the beginnings of what would capture my attention for the next two decades.

Another aspect of my life in the 1970s was the new friendships and partnerships I was forging at the time. By about 1963, I had joined a small consortium of like-minded and same-aged Japanese executives. In the United States, a company's board of directors consists of a selection of executives from various sectors of management in most cases. Every quarter or so, an American board meeting takes place so that the directors can discuss matters needing redirection or further definition. The executive director poses questions and sets the context for the members of the board. Garnering feedback from outside sources, especially those one respects and trusts, can yield amazing results.

Japanese board meetings are very different. The meeting is filled with executives and employees with a predetermined agenda. I frequently felt a sense that the walls were caving in a bit when I attended board meetings as Takihyo's president; the environment simply did not allow for any kind of spontaneity. Very few people shared fresh opinions, and no one was forced to solve problems on the fly. Everyone comes to these meetings prepared to discuss the matters on the current agenda—and *only* those matters. This form of problem solving can be stagnant at best, catastrophic at worst, because no one expresses any new ideas. These Japanese meetings are the opposite of American-style board meetings, where the objectivity of roundtable discussions brings fresh concepts from different perspectives. This was how the small group sessions in which I partook during consortium gatherings gave me a sounding board for some of my ideas, as well as a forum to learn from others' successes *and* mistakes.

This is not to say that the Japanese system doesn't have its advantages. Of course, Japanese board members are much more familiar with the company's problems than an executive who may be from another field or who may have another agenda. Moreover, because there is time before each meeting and the agendas are made known beforehand, Japanese executives can prepare potential solutions to some of the problems they will discuss. However, I yearned for something new at the time. Although I truly respected and trusted Takihyo's board members, they did not offer me everything that I needed as a young manager in rapidly changing times.

Kiyoshi Ichimura, president of what is now called the Ricoh Company, organized these consortium meetings; seven or eight members would meet in Tokyo once or twice a month to discuss business matters. The groups were small, so we all profited from the attention and feedback we could offer one another. The meetings proved fruitful both to our endeavors and to make room for more profound reflection on the issues at hand. Every couple of weeks, I eagerly took the train into Tokyo to attend another meeting and learn more about other industries and other management approaches. The meetings were a great experience; however, none of us felt as though we were giving ourselves enough exposure.

In the early 1970s, Japan really began to change. It was no longer a nation that lacked the luxuries of modern life. The Ministry of International Trade and Industry (MITI) in Japan began to open the doors to development not only domestically but abroad as well. Japan has always been a geographically small landmass—with an even smaller amount of usable land—in comparison to the United States and Western European countries. In the 1960s, the Japanese government worked very closely with the nation's banks to regulate any and all currency movement. If exchanges took place, the bank wanted to know exactly how much and for what purpose. However, circumstances couldn't remain this way if Japan was to experience any significant future growth, and policies changed by the 1970s. Originally, MITI was formed to protect and promote Japanese domestic industry. However, Japan was a nation in need of imports that did not have the resources to self-sustain without significant foreign trade agreements.

Once the Japanese government realized the necessity of outward-looking rather than inward-looking growth, Japanese tourism and business boomed. At this point, our small group of executives decided that we required some external support. We felt that the comments, criticisms, and questions of foreign managers could potentially offer us the perspectives to change business—not only in and for Japan but internationally as well. Because Japan was much smaller at the time, we all began thinking ahead in terms of our desire to expand our companies to service other areas—both domestically and overseas. We wanted every edge we could get; however, we needed contacts and connections in order to do this.

A writer for the weekly *Asahi* newspaper named Mr. Akai approached Ichimura, the leader of our consortium, and told him of the international group called the Young Presidents' Organization (YPO) that I mentioned in an earlier chapter. Ichimura then instructed Akai to learn about the organization, to find out who these young leaders were and if the group was on the same track as our small one. Shortly after, YPO sent some of their own delegates to Japan to meet with us. Given my previous exposure to English from working with a basketball coach at Keio and from the work I'd done with Bobbie

Brooks, I was thrust into the liaison position. The YPO members were impressed with us and approved the inception of a Japanese chapter right away. The only problem for us was that there weren't enough members; it really was just a few of us at the time.

Part of the problem in getting professionals to join our group had been the Japanese corporate climate during that period. There just weren't that many presidents in the young age group. Elderly individuals usually held the top managerial positions that would qualify someone to join YPO. Because the Japanese corporate climate at the time was primarily based on a system of seniority, we initially struggled to find people who fit the bill of young president. Luckily, there was a bit of a generation change that occurred during the 1960s and 1970s. Some of the elderly managers who were retiring encouraged young people to become presidents, and older people were kept on as chairs. Young presidents had therefore become a growing demographic by the mid-1970s.

Our numbers were not as strong as the American chapters, but we did not spare on the quality of our core membership. The executives we had gathered were some of the best and brightest in Japan, and our group's caliber brought prestige. Managers from around the nation wanted to join, which made the recruitment process a lot easier. This group's establishment marked my insertion into a network of individuals who changed my life. By the time I moved to the United States in the 1980s, I had not only friends in America, and around the world, but colleagues, business partners, and consultants as well—most of whom I'd met through the YPO conventions, which were called universities.

I became heavily involved with the organization from that point forward. While still fulfilling my duties as president of Takihyo, I'd been elected area vice president for YPO; the position allowed me to continue my work as liaison to the American headquarters. I was then obligated to attend board meetings overseas and at the YPO headquarters at least four times a year. Again, my companies in the United States and my previous exposure to practical conversational English put me in a different position than many other Japanese people. In most cases, the Japanese are proficient in reading and writing English; however, they lack English conversational skills. So in a way, I was willingly forced into my role with YPO.

Dreams

Kiyoshi Ichimura, who originally organized the consortium of young business leaders who met in Tokyo, and Ray Hickok shared the same dream. I first met Mr. Hickok in 1952, when he approached me with a consulting assignment. He wanted my company, BFS Psychological Associates, to evaluate a candidate for a position as his chief executive officer (CEO). I was recommended by a friend who was then an executive at the American Management Association. His name was Hensley Wedgwood of the famous Darwin family.

Ray shared his dream with me during our time together. He had inherited his father's belt company in Rochester, New York, upon his return from World War II, and he felt ill equipped to cope with the challenge. Then the question dawned on him: suppose *other* returning veterans were in the same boat—thrust into a responsibility for which they were not prepared? In the attempt to find a solution for this problem, Ray assembled a group of young, similarly inexperienced presidents—thereby giving birth to the YPO. It became Ray's passion. He spent so much time recruiting for new YPO members that he almost lost his belt business.

YPO now has chapters throughout the world. Although not a primary focus of this book, Tomio Taki's work with YPO is significant. Taki criticized the organization for calling itself international when he first joined, as YPO had only US, Canadian, and Mexican members. He was then on a mission to initiate conversations with businesspersons overseas—a mission that led to the establishment of a number of international YPO chapters. In his role as vice president of the organization, Tomio led the second (and perhaps largest) YPO conference in Tokyo with the largest committee—100 strong—YPO has ever seen. Taki was on track to become the first non-Caucasian president of the organization, but he had to rescind the invitation due to some of the problems Takihyo had been facing at the time.

(continued)

(continued)

I have lectured across the globe for YPO; it is where I met and became friendly with Tomio. Today, YPO is larger and stronger than ever. Now merged with the World President Organization, or WPO, the organization has 20,000 members in 100 countries.

Mortimer R. Feinberg, PhD

CHAPTER 10

The Lion

I have made some of my best friends through my involvement in the Young Presidents' Organization (YPO). In fact, it's how I met Mort Feinberg, the contributing sidebar editor of this book; he has lectured at numerous YPO events. The universities are usually held in large venues to accommodate 1,500 participants or more. Leaders from government and every industry present their opinions on current affairs. And although I am always interested in learning about how different business leaders confront various challenges, the most valuable lessons I've learned at YPO events have come from going to smaller, more informal forum meetings and cocktail hours. I don't drink myself, but I do attend these events to fraternize and network. I was always interested in these individuals' positions as international lecturers and members of YPO. Americans, in particular, have such dramatically divergent opinions on how to administrate and develop a company effectively.

It was through my YPO involvement, also, that I learned about the American fashion industry; because my YPO meetings obliged me to take a handful of annual trips to New York, I extended some of these stays to learn the ins and outs of the industry. Up until the 1980s when Japanese designers began to emerge as world leaders in fashion, there were few, if any, fashion-forward designers in Japan, and many Japanese took fashion cues from the West. The United States, on the other hand, had almost ubiquitous talent. After having worked with Bobbie Brooks, I reasoned that there was a great deal of opportunity in the United States for someone like me—ambitious, motivated, young, and most important, financed by an established textile manufacturing and distribution company. My Bobbie Brooks research had led me to implement a number of changes to Takihyo during the 1970s, since the existing methods we'd been using no longer made sense. Eventually, I became incredibly enthusiastic about the idea of manufacturing an American brand more inexpensively in the Far East. However, I needed to do much more research before I could fulfill my dream.

The first step was to find the right designer and brand with which to launch a joint venture—someone with whom I could see eye-to-eye. I had many ideas that I felt could be implemented across the industry, and I needed someone who would help me fulfill my vision. Timing was also essential to proper execution. I needed to move quickly; otherwise, the opportunity could pass me by. I therefore hired a number of my friends' American assistants—most of whom were young with fresh eyes and good taste—to conduct some guerrilla research. I thought they were good judges of fashion, and I wanted them to find brands that would give me a better feel for current US fashion trends.

I asked each assistant to take a day or two to shop alone. I wanted them to try on everything they liked. I didn't have them purchase anything; instead, I asked them to cut the hang-tags for every garment they wished they could own but couldn't necessarily afford. After a couple days of shopping, the young women brought me back a mountain of data—and the tags proved particularly fruitful. Newspapers, magazines, and my discussions with others in the business had been my main sources of fashion information; the tags my assistants collected offered me a fresh spin on consumer demand. This information allowed me, a foreigner, to feel the pulse of American fashion. Although there were many different design houses repre- sented by these tags, three names were the most ubiquitous—Bill

Blass, Roy Halston, and Anne Klein, and in that order. Surely, I reasoned, these designers were doing something better than the rest. So I arranged meetings with each of them in hopes of taking the next step forward.

I first met with Bill Blass, who had already established himself at the time. Having accrued five prestigious Coty American Fashion Critics' Awards for design, Blass's work garnered significant attention and he was well on his way to carving a place in American and international fashion history. My intentions for meeting with him were simple: I wanted to establish a joint venture with an American designer brand sportswear house to buy European materials, manufacture in the Far East, and distribute in the United States and Japan simultaneously. However, when I discussed these ideas with Blass, he said he was already overcommitted and couldn't partner with me. One down; two to go.

I met with Halston next; like Blass, he had a strong following. Some consider Halston one of the first designers to gain international acclaim as a designer. He is remembered today for his dressmaking and styling for some of America's most influential women: Jacqueline Kennedy Onassis, Liz Taylor, Liza Minnelli, and Lauren Bacall, to name just a few. Halston was also an icon of New York's fashion and party scene—and one who had an attitude to match his celebrity status. When I first walked into his office, I sat down across from Halston, introduced myself, and hoped to open a dialog. Halston picked up three oranges and started to juggle. Shortly thereafter, he called in his hairdresser for an impromptu haircut. Needless to say, he was less than serious about our meeting, and I left without forging a partnership.

The last designer with whom I met was Anne Klein, who was in her early 50s at the time. The Anne Klein Company was established in 1968. In contrast with Blass and Halston, Klein had less exposure—but despite her lesser acclaim, she was ahead of the curve as a designer. I liked what I saw of her lines. She had begun implementing mix-and-match and grouped products that were color-coordinated.

The Anne Klein Company had already incorporated separates into its small list of products, but Anne had no explicit reasoning for this line's lucrative potential. Her preliminary response was that her tacit knowledge appeared to coincide with my numerical deductions.

Although a tremendously creative person, Anne was also strong-minded and incredibly rational. She was the kind of woman who knew what she wanted and would work hard to achieve her goals. In this regard, we were very similar; although our means were different, we both aimed for the stars. Our first meeting was the start of a close corporate and personal relationship.

Anne was well on her to way to establishing a brand name by way of implementing some revolutionary concepts in the industry. First, Anne was intuitively aware of the basic sloper pattern-making technique. Whereas runway models are known for their minuscule waistlines and legs that go on for miles, most consumers don't possess such a physique. Making garments to fit runway models would make sense if everyone were 6 feet tall and weighed 100 pounds; however, according to the Centers for Disease Control and Prevention, the average woman in the United States is about 5 feet, 4 inches tall and weighs 165 pounds.[1] A basic sloper pattern scales a garment's bust and hip measurements to maintain a standard waist in all sizes. These patterns are drafted from house models—not from the runway models smattering fashion magazines—and are closer to the mean in size and proportion. Therefore, the waist sizes are more in sync with those of most consumers. Despite diet fads and current pop stars' looks, the female form has not changed very much over time. And fit is incredibly important to selling a garment. The magic of the basic sloper is that despite changes in styles, the sloper will stay the same. And with the right basic sloper, we could make any style fit.

Not everything was so easy, however. All joint ventures carry the possibility of various problems; this venture was no different. After crunching the numbers, I found that the partnership had limited profit potential. Buying materials mostly from Europe, shipping them to the Far East to manufacture, then transporting the finished goods to the United States were costly, especially considering all of the duties that were imposed on the garments. The outlook didn't look as rosy as I once thought it might.

For a while, I felt that my dream was crushed and that perhaps my business interests would have to remain on the other side of the Pacific. Anne, however, didn't want the joint venture opportunity to

[1]www.cdc.gov/nchs/fastats/bodymeas.htm.

disappear; she saw a lot of potential in what Takihyo could provide. So she asked me if I would buy into the company.

After taking a serious look at the financial figures for a joint venture, I was ready to leave the door open for future collaboration with Anne Klein. She truly surprised me with her offer; I'd had no idea the company was interested in selling equity. Although I was ecstatic, this solution brought other questions to the fore. I had initially wanted to enter a joint venture because I could not devote myself 100 percent to a new company. And I had little experience managing in the United States.

Anne Klein had incredible upside potential as a designer and as a business. The company was making money, but growth was stunted by a lack of fresh capital. Gunther Oppenheim, Anne's original business partner, put in his fair share. He not only invested money in the Anne Klein Company, but he also managed much of the business. However, I would not have been able to spend as much time on the venture as I would have liked if I were to invest. I would be forced to hire someone to be my eyes and ears, because I would be spending most of my time at Takihyo in Nagoya for the next seven years. I knew that doing this the right way required that I find the right employee.

Selecting the right kind of people for the positions they are to fill is essential to my managerial philosophy and integral for success. Hiring those individuals, however, is rarely an easy task. I have made many good decisions over the years, but that doesn't mean I haven't had my fair share of mistakes. I try to implement an age-old Buddhist teaching in management: "the skill in the liberative technique." Although I may not be able to emancipate individuals from the evils of worldly desire, I believe that I at least can help a person become successful. From what I have gathered, every employee appears to fit into one of four categories—and each category requires its own method via which to make the subordinate an asset rather than a liability.

First, there is the model employee. I believe every employee can be molded and shaped into a person who can be given instructions and execute efficiently; sometimes, however, this takes time and experience. The model employee understands the superior's intentions and implements directives properly even if there are gaps in the initial explanations. The model employee asks questions when matters are unclear without fear of rejection or demoralization. There is no ego on the job; only reason and the directives provided. I try to challenge and nurture the employees I hire who reach or have reached this point in their careers. I also try to hold on to this kind of person as long as possible.

The second type of employee is one who understands directives but fails in the execution. There are a multitude of reasons why someone may fit into this category; however, the main factor is usually that nothing precipitated from the directions given. In most cases, managers have to handle these employees differently. Perhaps this person isn't in the right position, or maybe he or she no longer values his or her position. In most cases, the former scenario is easier to handle. Managers can ask employees what they would really like to do and then work together to try to make it happen. The latter, however, is a different story altogether. If an employee doesn't care anymore about the company—or at least about his or her job—management should likely let that person go.

As a Japanese businessperson, I try my best to adhere to my native custom of lifetime employment. However, if there is no "right" place for an employee, he or she has to go. I have always attempted to put myself somewhere between the American's ease to pull the trigger and the Japanese view of supporting employees no matter what and continuing to push them to succeed—even if they resist. There are no easy answers to handling this type of employee.

A third type of employee is one who doesn't understand directions—and fails to follow through as a result. These employees are as easy to spot as the second type; they merely lack the attitude. Therefore, if a manager repeats the same commands in a way that is easier to understand, this third type will most likely execute the task effectively. Sometimes, people need directions framed in different ways for the overall picture to make more sense. People all think and act differently—which is something that we as managers need to take into account when administering directives. More often than not, these employees fear being rejected or having a boss label them as stupid or inept. They don't ask questions; and consequently, they don't succeed. Yet once they receive adequate training, these kinds of employees may transform into the ideal, model employee.

The fourth type of employee represents the most dangerous and potentially destructive employee: those who do not understand directives but instead act blindly. Managers need to make sure every employee is on—or at the very least, *around*—the same page; otherwise, severe damage can occur. This type of employee may initially appear like the model employee; however, he or she usually does not ask the right questions and/or does not see the purpose of the given instructions. Managers may want to give these people increasing responsibility within the company; eventually, however, the false image of this employee's work is revealed. By and large, once this occurs, it is too late to amend the damage, and managers have to carry forward with whatever losses were incurred.

Of course, there is plenty of gray area, and the different employee types often overlap within an individual. Other problems with these definitions emerge in regard to the difference between those who can be incredibly successful in large corporate structures and those who work more effectively in smaller operations. Van Isaacs, for example, matured as a businessperson in the largest of fashion houses, yet found himself running a small mom-and-pop operation later in life (that I bought from a tailor called the Tailored Sportsman). Isaacs was comfortable as the executive of a large fashion company, but he did not excel when he started focusing his energies on a much smaller operation.

Another stumbling block is culture. In Japan, for instance, there are 17 ways to say "yes" but mean "no." Nodding—particularly in Western nations—unequivocally means "yes"; but in the Far East, it's a knee-jerk response to inform the speaker that he or she is being heard. I routinely ask my Japanese employees what my previous directives were and have them repeat in their own words what I have asked them to accomplish. Yet when I have done this in the United States, employees sometimes think I am demeaning or ridiculing them. However, I make sure that if there are any comments, criticisms, or questions to the instructions, everyone acknowledges what they are so that we all can work with one another without any administrative or logistical hiccups.

Although there are always exceptions, the way I have learned to categorize my employees has been largely effective—if somewhat crude. Having a general outline for viewing different types of employees prompts how I change, instruct, and direct subordinates. This overview has provided me with an integrated approach to handling problems—based not only on subjective traits but also on anthropological and sociological ones. However, there's one golden rule that always holds true: to be effective across international lines, a manager needs to keep his or her ego in check. When employees become defensive and fearful, the environment is not right for them—and the wrong environment leads only to future mistakes, misfortune, and miscommunication. One of the most important elements of management is picking the right subordinates; that way, one has less to manage!

I first met Bob Oliver of Anne Klein at one of the many YPO functions I attended. Oliver is one of the craftiest people I have encountered. When confronted with a problem, he would jump over the fence rather than walk to the distant door. He had a special ability to weigh his options quickly and then take the path of least resistance. Some conservative businesspersons may view Oliver as teetering on the edge of some ethical lines, but I thought his skill set was priceless. In addition, I wanted him to do only temporary work for me.

Oliver made sense as a hire because I needed someone who could argue the price down for my stake in the Anne Klein Company. Although Anne wanted to work with me, she also had a very shrewd fashion-industry guru behind her. Gunther Oppenheim, an original financier for the Anne Klein Company as well as for Dior and other brands, knew how much to invest in designers, and I needed the leverage an outsider could provide without damaging any relationships. As I've mentioned before, the 1970s were a challenging decade in Japan; I had to spend a lot of time dealing with the disruptions at Takihyo as well as a great deal of personal loss. I didn't have the luxury of paying much attention to the minutiae at Anne Klein initially. I could focus only on broad strokes, so I needed someone on the inside I could trust. I therefore decided to temporarily hire Oliver to be my American eyes and ears.

I put Bob Oliver in a position to handle my discussions with Anne Klein and Gunther from the first negotiations. I chose him because of his personality and willingness to take initiative. Oliver was mild-mannered, and I needed to build bridges rather than burn them. Oliver negotiated my concessions for Anne and Gunther while arguing down my price for equity in the Anne Klein Company. I was also spending quite a bit of time in Japan so if a question needed answering, I could trust Oliver to give me the appropriate information to make the right decisions.

Leadership Styles

There was a time in the bad old days when the only form of motivation known to a businessperson was to get bigger and better whips. Now, of course, brute force is frowned upon. A businessperson would probably lose his or her credentials in the American Management Association—and be served with a sentence—if he or she so much as laid a hand on a subordinate.

So what do we use nowadays instead of bigger whips? A lot of people would say we use psychology. When it's used this way, the word *psychology* carries more or less the connotation of "being nice." You must establish rapport.

But *rapport* is still quite a broad term, so let's narrow it down. There has been a good bit of discussion of leadership style for the manager recently. The question of whether he or she should be an autocratic or democratic leader has been posed. The answer is obvious for most people—and for most executives: being democratic is far preferable to taking an autocratic approach. The values of democracy are part of our national and cultural heritage. We prize freedom; we scorn dictators and autocrats.

Translated into management terms, the democratic style of leadership has come to mean that we emphasize the importance of understanding people as human beings; we give them a high degree of freedom in the working environment and accomplish objectives through persuasion and understanding, rather than through close supervision and giving orders.

In this chapter, we see Taki delegate a vast amount of responsibility to Bob Oliver. Some may consider what he did crazy, whereas others tend to think he made the best possible management decision he could have made. Here, Taki implemented a leadership style very much akin to what Hitotsubashi University professor Hiro Takeuchi calls knowledge creation—a situation in which an executive gives broad strokes, and the employee details the fine lines. Taki exemplifies this non–Western approach that seems to work well in the Western world. However, he still

(continued)

(continued)

adheres to what I consider an integrated approach to imprinting the employee.

Taki was candid about his objectives with Oliver and told him what he wanted to come out of the negotiations with Anne Klein and Gunther Oppenheim. He oriented Oliver in a way that was best designed to accomplish the goals at hand and therefore granted Oliver even greater security and an immediate feeling of understanding and respect for Taki. This process seems to underscore the four steps involved in securing one's leadership role:

1. Immediately imprint your policy, authority, and style on subordinates.

2. Evaluate the degree to which you are establishing yourself with the employee.

3. Estimate the tenure of the key individuals who will be carrying out your program.

4. Appraise your training plan according to the desired approach.

Mortimer R. Feinberg, PhD

CHAPTER 11

Negotiating for Anne Klein

As I mentioned briefly in the previous chapter, I hired Bob Oliver to negotiate a partnership agreement with Anne Klein and Gunther Oppenheim for equity in the Anne Klein Company. These conversations went on for about a year before we were able to close the deal and confirm my position as president on behalf of Takihyo Company Ltd. in October 1973. The transaction left Anne and Gunther each with 25 percent of the Anne Klein Company. I held a 50 percent stake, giving Takihyo Company Ltd. majority equity and freeing me as a manager to implement any necessary changes quickly and effectively. Although the Anne Klein Company had a solid customer base and was earning a fair amount, there were also gross inefficiencies. After completing an analysis during the process of purchasing Takihyo's stake, I knew the different areas in which I had to streamline and tone the Anne Klein Company.

When I get involved in a new endeavor, I want to know how information traverses the corporate structure. I enjoy digging up inconsistencies and finding solutions. Therefore, I wanted to learn more about the nuts and bolts of the business when I first arrived in the

United States and began my conversations with Anne and Gunther. I wanted to see how everything in the company worked: from the way that management treated subordinates to how distribution and warehousing functioned. Even if Anne Klein was on its way to becoming a name brand in the field, I did not want to take on debt—or a company that I couldn't grow. I knew that I would probably need to make significant changes to the organization; however, I wanted to know where, how, and how long it would probably take before signing the final agreements. These points helped also in amassing a list that Oliver could use as ammunition when negotiating price.

In some instances, problems arose that I had never anticipated. For example, I had never before encountered the "not-my-job" syndrome. One of my first visits to Anne Klein's packing and shipping division opened my eyes and allowed me to see how different Japanese and American companies are. Although I like to believe people are more similar than different, cultural differences are incredibly acute in some areas. There are no unions in Japan, nor is there a significant division between the importance of the sales associate and the executive manager. Of course, there is something of a top-down structure that includes incentive and pay differences, but most of the decisions are made by middle management. Companies, however, act more like unions rather than divisions. Japanese employees have an allegiance to the company and endeavor to find ways to make it better—because the company's profitability is directly tied to employee performance. If a company prospers, managers and subordinates do too.

However, unions in the United States have rooted themselves in nearly every industry. The Anne Klein distribution center had pickers and packers. The packers would take goods from one side of the warehouse to the other for processing; the pickers would select the garments off the rack, then give them to the packers for shipping. The packers were represented by one workers' union, and the pickers were considered a separate arm of that union. As per union negotiations, there were to be a certain number of pickers and packers in the warehouse during operating hours.

Although I had previously read about how labor unions worked in the United States, I didn't quite grasp the union-worker mentality. After making general observations of the warehousing operation at Anne Klein for about 5 minutes, I asked one of the workers why he was sitting around, listening to music and drinking coffee, watching others hard at work. To my chagrin, he commented, "Shippers move the inventory after the packers pack it"—then went back to doing nothing. In this case, the separate unions offered no incentive for building a sense of collaboration in the workplace. The shippers were members of a different union than the packers—and neither had an allegiance to the company that employed them. These people cared only about their unions. Even if the company paid the bills, the union had alienated this worker from the very task at hand. This example illustrates how performance does not necessarily have a tight-knit relationship with compensation. Aside from the complacency that these unions had institutionalized at Anne Klein, an us versus them dichotomy had emerged. One union's workers did only one job, while another union's workers did only another. There was no cooperation; therefore, two different tasks or projects—in this particular case, packing and shipping—took more time and cost more money than if everyone were working together, for the company and not for the union. This "it's-not-my-job" attitude harms so many companies.

While the shipper exemplified this attitude, implicit rifts had emerged in the communication and commitment to the company's greater aim—conflicts that I felt compelled to address. Larger companies have found ways to change the union mentality more recently. Toyota, for example, continued to hire employees; but instead of hiring task-specific workers from a car painting union or an assembly union (these particular unions may not actually exist, but I use them for illustrative purposes), the company would assign a group of employees to produce a certain number of cars. Many American auto companies have endured slow and unprofitable production processes because cars cannot be shipped without doors or bumpers if that particular group goes on strike. I applaud Toyota for taking the approach it has; the company has brought once-unionized employees one step closer to having an allegiance to their company.

There was little I could do to change labor unions in the fashion industry, but there were many flaws in the original incarnation of the Anne Klein Company that I could address. The company was doing well, but there were unnecessary divisions that needed to be consolidated. A company cannot run without open communication. In this case, merchandising needed financial management. Any and every choice that the design team makes has repercussions in the company's financial planning and vice versa. Even if the company's designers are the most brilliant in the world, if they are given free rein to spend for each and every line, the company will end up bankrupt. Therefore, although Anne Klein had a positive bottom line, there were inefficiencies bleeding the company of capital because of a lack of communication.

At times, fashion companies' financial arms make executive decisions that infringe upon the design team's preferences—and these misunderstandings can unravel fashion companies. Nothing gets accomplished if these two groups cannot work together. Therefore, the first change I made to Anne Klein was to integrate financial management and accounting divisions with the design and merchandising teams. I felt very strongly about the fact that everyone needed to be on the same page. These groups endured the same kind of division that the shippers and packers did, and they also disregarded the organization that supported their livelihoods. I wanted to reduce these misunderstandings by highlighting how success in the fashion industry necessitates constant attention and collaboration across disciplines rather than against one another. I wanted every one of my employees to work together; I wanted the budgeting department to keep merchandising's needs in mind and the design team to consider the accounting team's preferences.

For instance, sometimes certain garments would not reach the department stores at the same time as others from the same collection. Moreover, the department stores try to sell the clothing at discount at the end of every season—thereby hurting their profitability and decreasing the size of the next season's order. Although it's nearly impossible to sell an entire season's worth of clothing, I wanted to find a working solution to increase sales for goods that were not the first to leave the racks and for those that came later in the season.

Designer fashion covers four seasons of clothing over the course of the year: transitions between spring/summer, summer/fall, fall/winter, and a holiday line and/or a resort line of clothing. I wanted to coordinate the tail end of the previous season with the upcoming season at Anne Klein so that we could sell both seasons simultaneously. Department stores return goods that aren't sold at the end of the season—a practice I wanted to limit. Displaying new goods next to those from the previous season—and selling them in a coordinated fashion—would not only allow consumers to have a greater choice in the look they wished to achieve but also give the manufacturer, distributor, and department stores more opportunity to sell the goods. After all, no one likes to take 5 percent when 15 percent net margin is possible.

Anne Klein's marketing team didn't like this idea, though; they wanted each season to have a stark change from one to the other. They had a point; the changeover lines give consumers a perspective on seasons. However, the majority of the garments produced were of weights suitable for only two seasons (fall and spring), and marketing didn't realize how much this crisp change was costing the company. The methods they were employing also put the department stores in a bad position; they then had to sell at a discount to the recommended retail price. Selling at clearance then came back to hurt us. It caused us to receive a smaller order the following season or year or prompted department stores to offer us our percentage of the goods sold at clearance and not retail prices. Either scenario hurt our bottom line.

My approach challenged the way in which buyers and suppliers treated clothing at the department stores. Although it was unconventional, coordinating design of the ends and beginnings of each season's line kept merchandise in stores longer and gave consumers more choices to mix and match garments. Not only did Anne Klein increase its profitability as a result, but the department stores did as well. Consumers were also happier because of the increased opportunity to match pieces from last season with the current season's offerings, which offered new, coordinated looks. If, for example, a consumer found only a top that she liked, but no bottom, she might not buy the top. However, if she came back at the beginning of the following season to find that the top she liked was still available along with a new bottom that she preferred over previous offerings, the department store might then have a sale.

Although it might be easier to form a business partnership than to launch a company from scratch, an existing business also has its challenges. I have made a point in each of my new partnerships to seek out any existing flaws and make all attempts to ensure that the organization doesn't repeat these mistakes in the future. Missteps will inevitably happen; however, when an issue arises, I want everyone to convene and come up with the right solutions—in unison. Emphasizing the need for lateral communication from one department to another can also open doors for employees. Accounting specialists can become creative with merchandising to find new, economical means by which to sell/show products. Financial planners and executives can home in on some of the decisions made by the design team to manufacture fewer samples and be more selective with materials to limit creative costs (which can skyrocket if left unchecked). Managing a company requires that one use the conflicts and questions of one division to attempt to solve the conflicts and questions of another's.

Establishing Yourself

Although there is little a manager can do about unions and their requirements, there are ways to push subordinates to get the bigger picture. Frequently, whenever someone new comes into a position of authority within a company, that person tends to talk about change. And although change can be stimulating, it can also be threatening. To win the fullest enthusiasm and cooperation possible from staff, a manager's efforts must maximize positive stimulation and minimize the threat of difference. Three elements are most important in this situation: personal enthusiasm, effective communication, and selective job structuring.

As Tomio points out, unions in the fashion industry appear to control processing, receiving, and shipping; in the office, however, separate divisions have respective objectives. The budgeting department and the merchandising teams were working to accomplish different tasks. Budgeting was conscious of only the earnings-to-expenses ratio, whereas merchandising was interested only in making the product look its best. Tomio recognized that a company needs to have a unified vision; and each individual, regardless of division, must take part in creating the company's vision. His consolidation of the budgeting and merchandising divisions aligned both short- and long-term aims of what were once two separate parts of the organization. Tomio revamped the ways in which employees viewed challenges; it wasn't just about how to make the product look a certain way anymore, but also how to make it cost-effective. This simple integration of divisions not only helped Anne Klein save money but also brought more employees on the same page and introduced new, stimulating challenges for Tomio's subordinates.

Mortimer R. Feinberg, PhD

CHAPTER 12

Losing a Friend

Four and a half months after I'd purchased half of the Anne Klein Company, Anne died of breast cancer. Everyone was devastated. I had not only lost a new friend but lost the heart and soul of my new business. Although I had been aware of Anne's previous battle with cancer, both Anne and her oncologists assured me that the disease was in remission. She hadn't appeared sick, and the doctors encouraged her to continue her normal routine. However, the doctors couldn't have been more wrong.

When I first bought into the company, Anne and I would talk every day. There was always a problem to solve, whether it was in the design room or the core business. Bob Oliver was helping me make a few structural changes to the company, and Anne wanted to remain in the loop. She helped transition the operations from where they were to where they could be, and she also called me just to talk about what was going on in her personal life. Anne's death brought an unfortunate end to a friendship and a partnership.

Although I felt a bit overwhelmed upon losing both a close friend and a business associate, I didn't have much time to mourn. The deadlines for the upcoming season were fast approaching—and we did not have a chief designer. The Anne Klein Company had invested a lot of money in samples and materials already, and there was no way I was going to abandon the brand. Anne had built up an image for the company; I would not let her effort be for naught. After her death, there was still her legacy, not only in the ideas but also in the very designs that had initially attracted me to the company. So my partners and I went back to the drawing board.

The company was well on its way to establishing a big-name brand. Anne the designer had begun to accrue almost celebrity status within the industry while amassing a strong consumer base. Unlike today, designers in the 1970s were known less by the media and more by the industry's inner circles; nevertheless, many people, both in the industry and among the public, had begun to link the name *Anne Klein* with *elegant* and *timeless* design. The momentum was there; we just had to figure out how to handle Anne's succession. It was a matter that significantly increased contention in the boardroom.

Chip Rubenstein—Anne's widower, who inherited a quarter of the company—and Gunther Oppenheim wanted a big-name designer to assume the mantle. I am not sure how much Chip had influenced Anne's designs; however, I did know that Gunther had been there only as a business partner. Although Gunther had accomplished a great deal as a very respected figure in the fashion world, his involvement had been limited in terms of the ideas Anne and I had exchanged concerning the brand's growth. After Anne's death, both Gunther and Chip wanted a high-profile designer to assume control. However, I knew that difficulties always arise whenever a new creative element is added into the mix. Furthermore, the costs associated with hiring new, trusted talent can be prohibitive. Although it seemed risky from Gunther and Chip's point of view, I suggested promoting the assistant designer because she had worked closely with Anne for the last few years.

Chip and Gunther disagreed with this approach. However, we all knew that I would be the one to suffer the most if the wrong successor was chosen. I owned 50 percent of the company, and therefore I had the most skin in the game. As a result, I needed to take a different angle with my partners to convince them that the assistant was a better option than hiring someone else and starting from scratch for the upcoming line. I knew I had to develop my thesis, so I racked my brains to develop a system to quantify design talent for the express purpose of comparing Chip and Gunther's choices to my own.

The situation's urgency was great, and I had a lot of arguments with Chip and Gunther over choosing the right successor. Because I didn't know all that much about the American design scene, I had no idea who would be the best. However, I wanted to take my weakness and transform it into a strength. Designers today may scoff at what I did, but at the time it made perfect sense to me as a businessperson. Accountants would not consider a designer an item on a company's balance sheet; however, the designer's creativity is an intangible asset worth much more than the company's stated book value. If we could earn $10 the previous year and $15 this year—and forecast that we will earn at least $15 or more every year over the next 10 years due to innovative design—the designer and his or her longevity would be worth much more than staid cash on a balance sheet accruing interest.

But how can you put a price on creativity? How do you measure talent? Anne had a number of awards that set her apart from the crowd. However, the awards did not make Anne who she was. The accolades she received from her peers were applause for past deeds—not for future ingenuity and progress in design. Therefore, the only way to determine talent was to refer to my developing notions of consumer taste and desire. Consequently, I reduced fashion design to four broad elements: color, design, material, and fit. These four elements do not account for the personality or work ethic of the designer; they merely provide insight into a designer's approach.

Color, design, material, and fit also carry the sensory element's contribution to the overall appeal of a garment. These design factors track a consumer's receptivity from the moment she walks into the store until she leaves—regardless of whether a final sale is made. Taken together, these four elements have a different effect on what I like to call the profit-building value of a fashion brand. I have measured this quality in many different ways: the concept and design behind Stacy Ames, the brand mentioned earlier in the book, held an immense profit-building value. There was almost no Western-style women's wear in Japan at the time. Therefore, this division had a built-in moat that protected it from outside competition; it offered something different from what everyone else was offering. Although the cost of entry was low for large distributors and manufacturers, the Japanese garment industry wasn't ready for sweeping changes. No one believed Japanese women would take to Western clothing with such zeal, despite the fact that Japanese men had been wearing Western-style clothing since the late nineteenth century. Women, many people assumed, are the keepers of culture and tradition; those unwilling to make the leap into the unknown believed Japanese women would be resistant to change. However, these people were wrong—and Takihyo reaped the benefits from its contrarian position.

A fashion company's profit-building value can provide a rough estimate for the designer's fair market value as a human, creative asset to the company. Stacy Ames, for example, held value in a place where there was no established market for what we were offering. I had to think about what consumers really desired in order to understand this concept. Although clothing lines differ from one creator to the next, it all boils down to two primary components: design and emotional value. A marquee-name designer would deliver this kind of necessary emotional value to Anne Klein. Chip and Gunther wanted this built-in value, since a designer's reputation can do wonders for elevating a brand's status. However, a designer's stature can come at a hefty price that includes monetary compensation as well as having to manage an already well-inflated ego. I hoped instead to uncover and nurture talent in Anne's assistant; these are always the most efficient means for growing a business. An already established designer may have hit the ceiling for his or her popularity, whereas a fresh, new face has a larger margin of safety—especially if he or she has room to develop. The system I developed to compare designers—both marquee names and Anne's assistant—was meant to facilitate the decision-making process.

As previously discussed, color, design, material, and fit comprised the four major elements in our structure. Each one carries its own weight in terms of its importance to the quantification of the profit-building value inherent in the designers Chip and Gunther had brought before me. Color, for example, takes a 30 percent stake, since consumers notice color before any other factor. If a garment's hue pops or is more attractive in some way, the consumer heads back to the rack. Color serves as the first hook, the teaser, the invitation to the brand. It needs to satisfy consumers' particular desires, no matter how subjective, and meet demands that range from standing out to blending in. An eye for color is a talent less common than others, so it has to be just right—otherwise, a sale will not be made.

Whereas color initiates a dialog with the eye, fabric does so with the consumers' touch. Consumers notice the fabric after seeing the garment, thereby expanding sensory input. A fabric may be comforting, cozy, functional, sensual—and anything in between and beyond. Again—what appeals to the consumer is entirely subjective. A garment's material is also critical and can make or break a sale. When confronted with what textiles to use and how to use them, designers frequently opt to custom-make fabrics. A good designer will use a quality fabric to increase the product's desirability. Touch, however, is much more reproducible than color. Although color is far more important, the feel of a garment's material generates a substantial 20 percent of the profit-building value.

Many assume that creativity is at the crux of what makes a great fashion company; however, I disagree. So many great designers are out there, but very few have married great style to profitable margins. Creativity in design is important, but it is perhaps the least important in terms of what determines the profitability of a fashion house. The value that a good designer can bring to the table lasts only as long as that designer remains a celebrity. If a designer cannot add something extra special to the product line, he or she risks fading in importance—and eventually falling off of the consumer radar.

Consumers are also very fickle. Even a designer who is trendy today might be old news by tomorrow. Out of the four elements of profit-building value, originality in design ranks lowest on the scale, since there is no way to predict whether a new and innovative design will catch the public's eye. Although design may be the final deciding factor for a consumer, it is also the most subjective; therefore, it generates only 10 percent in my profit-building value thesis.

Although color and material are very important factors, and design a somewhat important element, fit trumps them all in my theory of profit-building value. Color, material, and design lure customers to try on garments, but the 20 minutes or so that they spend in the dressing room and around the store are the true moments of judgment. If a garment does not fit properly or appears unflattering, the sale simply won't happen. Even if a tailor can alter an otherwise beautiful dress for $10, most consumers do not think past the dressing room. Moreover, those kinds of alterations are not only a hassle but impractical for most consumers. It makes no sense for a customer to purchase a dress from Company X that does not fit, when Company Y offers something comparable that is much more flattering and fits beautifully. A proper fit is a critical part of any clothing-buying decision. Close to half of all potential sales are either made or lost in the dressing room—a fact that not every designer understands. This means that clothes not only have to fit the runway models, but, more importantly, have to fit women of different shapes and sizes. A fashion line needs to accommodate the mother of three as well as the young professional woman. A designer needs to know what consumers want—what makes them feel most comfortable or professional and attractive. Fit is the deal clincher, and therefore takes 40 percent of the profit-building value.

I proposed this system to Chip and Gunther as a stab at quantitative analysis. We then went over each of the 25 designers on our list, assigned each individual a value from 1 to 10, and then weighted each according to my system. According to this test, a clear winner emerged: Donna, Anne's previous assistant. Chip and Gunther both acknowledged that based on our three separate scores, Donna was the best choice; however, they were still not comfortable hiring the assistant.

Because I held a majority equity position, I had the most to lose if choosing Donna proved to be a mistake. However, Gunther and Chip would be along for the ride; and according to their line of thought, their current holdings would evaporate if I were to hire Donna. When I told them I thought Donna had what it took, Gunther bowed out of our partnership. He took considerable gains from his investment and walked away from the Anne Klein Company. Chip, on the other hand, decided to stick around for a little while longer in hopes that I had made the right decision.

Making the Right Decisions About People

The most important decisions that most managers make are about people. You hire people, you promote people, and sometimes, you have to fire people. Every one of these decisions can have a profound effect on the way your operation runs and on your own ability to receive a promotion to a better job. If you can improve your batting average on decisions regarding people by even a modest amount, you'll be a better manager—and a more relaxed one too. For when managers are constantly battling situations in which they are trying to solve the puzzles presented by a diversity of human beings, their tension gauge often quivers near the breaking point.

We have grown wary of seat-of-the-pants decisions in this age of information. Most managers are able to put together a mass of data that more or less bear upon all their choices—particularly those affecting staff assignments. However, like Tomio's first instinct to hire Donna—which he then proved by quantifying the profit-building value that was inherent in each of the prospective designers—*your* first instinct may very well lead you to make the best decision possible.

Researchers are probing deeply into this mysterious matter of instinct. Ethnologists have studied the habit patterns of animals and come up with valuable insights into the human condition. There is growing evidence that instinctive reactions should be given greater weight than we have traditionally accorded to them. This is not to say you should act impulsively; you want to gather enough facts to check out your instinctive reaction. But don't forget it or discard it out of hand. We are learning that instinct is not aberration. The hunch that tells you, "This is the man to promote," may be the result of an extremely complex process that's taking place in your subconscious. We have a lot to learn about instinct; however, it does appear that, when faced with a challenge, the mind—in a computer-like

(continued)

(continued)

fashion—swiftly sums up the accrued product of years of experience and observation to suggest the best possible answer.

We are not, however, aware of the process—only the result, or hunch, that pops up unbidden. And, of course, we know that not all hunches are fully worthy of trust. Thus, we too often throw out the baby with the bathwater. We are so suspicious of the very instinct that we often deliberately take a course opposite to that indicated by the hunch.

However, don't do it! You can make the decision process easier *and* more rational by giving serious consideration to your instinctive reaction to a situation. Write your hunch down and then flesh it out. Ask yourself tough questions about it. If there is no immediate and obviously crippling drawback that becomes apparent, go further. Collect information, but don't get carried away. Gather facts that have a real bearing on the decision. If your initial feeling seems to check out, then you may well find that it is the best course for you to take. A growing amount of scientific experimentation indicates that this is so. We are learning that our hunches are often mental "printouts" based on years of input, weighted and calculated by the finest of all computers—the human brain.

Mortimer R. Feinberg, PhD

CHAPTER 13

Finding New Management

After buying out Gunther, I needed to find qualified help. Although Chip had declared himself a managing partner, he was not qualified for the job. I don't believe he had ever managed a company before— something that caused a number of internal problems. Managing the crises in Japan as well as a growing fashion company in the United States was too much responsibility for me alone. I wanted to delegate the logistical operations and the maintenance areas of management, but I needed the right person to fill that role. So far, Bob Oliver had been helping, but I couldn't kid myself; there was no way he would or could take on the position of president or chief officer of operations. Oliver had his own matters to which he had to attend. Therefore, my last request of him was to help in the search for someone new to be my eyes and ears on US soil and help run the Anne Klein Company.

I didn't have too much time, but it was important that I find someone I could trust to handle such a large investment. I needed a full-time manager with some experience to help build the business according to my vision. Since I had little exposure to American fashion, I didn't know where to begin looking. I asked Oliver for a good headhunter, and he directed me to Ken Langstaff from Ward Howell International.

I would have preferred to interview a long list of potential candidates, but I could not. I had to trust Ken's, then Oliver's judgment. Ken sent Oliver a list of potential prospects, from which Oliver chose three or four names, all of whom had a significant amount of experience in the garment business. I had in mind someone on the young side but with strong managerial skills. As far as I was concerned, experience was a part of the past; I wanted *new* thinking in order to develop fresh concepts. I was looking for candidates with both compelling credentials and excellent managerial skills—and I put great stock in the chemistry between the candidate and myself. I knew there was no way it would work if we couldn't get along.

Oliver suggested that I meet the most appealing candidate first. I had to get back to Japan quickly, and it wasn't an option for me to fly to the East Coast where the prospect, Frank Mori, worked at the time. So, since I enjoyed playing golf as much as I could, Oliver organized a round of golf for the three of us in San Francisco.

Frank had a stellar educational background; he had earned a BA from Dartmouth College and an MBA from Harvard University. Frank also had good work experience. He had worked at the executive level handling marketing at the Dixie Cup division of General Mills and at Bali Bras. Although he had little experience as a chief executive, he was young, bright, and willing to learn. There were gaps in his knowledge, but I was comfortable with his level of skill. I hurriedly flew back to Japan after a brief discussion with Oliver, but I knew that I had made my decision after that meeting.

Oliver called Ken Langstaff to inform him of our decision; unfortunately, Ken had just had a heart attack. Whether it was related to the tough times or merely a health issue, I don't know, but Oliver relayed the information about Frank's new position before Ken's hospitalization. After a successful surgery, Frank visited Ken at the hospital to find out the good news. After taking care of a few things in Japan, I returned to the United States and began to sort out my agreement with Frank. It was a short meeting, but I cemented what would become a long friendship and partnership.

What I needed from Frank was not generally what one asks of a newly hired executive. Most executives are hired and then trained for the job. However, I didn't really have the time to take Frank through all the steps. I wanted Frank to know that I trusted him, and I wanted his interests to align with my own. Being on the same page was absolutely necessary, so whenever I was not in the United States, I would make sure that Frank would consult me regarding any necessary fundamental changes. However, Frank was more or less on his own at times right from the start; I trusted that I could give him the ball and let him run with it.

I treated Frank as if he had been there all along and knew how to run the company. I prefer to give full control rather than limit one's judgment—perhaps a result of my management experience in the Far East. Frank clearly had talent; as a manager, I have learned that the best growth occurs when the subordinate has more rather than less responsibility and when errors have some kind of proportionate relationship with the amount that one can learn. Frank had been stuck in a marketing placement at General Mills and at Bali's. Those kinds of boundaries don't make sense to me; if someone does well in a particular area but has no knowledge of how the rest of the business functions, the production or merchandising arms can still fail—even if marketing is done well. I wanted to give Frank room to show me his capabilities. This management style also provided me with the flexibility I needed until I could uproot my life to move to New York. One game of golf—four hours on a course—was my basis for hiring Frank; that meeting opened the doors for a relationship that has lasted until this day. Some people might think it a risky move to hire someone for such a high position after spending so little time with him; however, I believe that golf is the ultimate leveler. Although four hours may not be that long in the real world, it is enough time— as well as the perfect environment—in which to observe how one handles frustration and intense anxiety.

I viewed the game as a psychological test for Frank—a way to view his inner workings without asking him questions. Sometimes, when asked, the listener gives tailored responses regardless of the truth. I like to believe that people always tell the truth; however, that's not always the case, especially if it is not in the respondent's best interest. It's never a good idea to ask difficult questions of someone you just met, especially if the answers are important. Therefore, I used the game of golf as a tool for psychological analysis.

Interviewees expect a dialog to inform their understanding of whether or not they will be hired. However, I didn't want words to obfuscate. I knew that observing how one plays golf unveils quirks and idiosyncrasies—because of how emotionally trying the sport can be. Of course, not every manager is a great golfer. And great golfers come about only with a lot of experience and practice. However, good managers tend to act and react somewhat similarly on the course.

Anxiety, frustration, and impatience are the three most difficult emotions; and as any golfer can attest, these ugly feelings emerge frequently in the sport. Observing how the prospective executive handles difficulties in the game will give you a good idea of how he or she will control these same emotions when running a business. Does the person get angry quickly? Poor anger management can result in alienating potential clients and subordinates. In addition, the way in which a golfer manages frustration tells a lot about how he or she will manage others. How does the individual react to short-term failure? How well does this person concentrate? How much does he or she care about performance?

I noticed during our first meeting that Frank was very intent on playing the game and very serious about the rules and etiquette. His score was not doctored up with mulligans, but rather by a stroke-by-stroke recount of each hole. The strictness by which he followed the rules would extend to arguing his position through the USGA rules in the case of a dispute. He uses a similar approach in the way he's come to handle legal issues regarding managerial decisions. This insight led me to conclude that if an issue were to arise, Frank would most likely argue minutiae to get the best results—not only for himself but for the company as well. Although I am not a psychologist, I have grown to understand the areas in which people can be predictable, and I use it to my advantage.

Intuition and Placement

General George C. Marshall advised his colleagues to develop people toward self-reliance. "If you want a man to be for you," he said, "never let him feel he is dependent on you. Make him feel *you* are in some way dependent on *him*." And the best way to do that is to teach him to stand on his own feet. This is what Tomio Taki did with Frank Mori. Not knowing what the future would hold for him, Taki made a gut decision to hire Frank to help build what would become a very lucrative investment. Without offering much more than an introduction, Tomio thrust Frank into the president's office at the Anne Klein Company. It's incredibly difficult to quantify the value in Taki's hunch, but one thing is certain: the best leaders in business use and rely on their instincts on a regular basis.

Studies on the brain suggest that the left hemisphere is the locus of our logical, sequential, rational, and verbal processes, whereas the right side is the organ for intuitive, imaginative, artistic, and creative processes. Despite all the attention given to rationalism in management literature and education, a study by Harry Mintzberg of McGill University has suggested that chief executive officers (CEOs) in leading companies actually use the right side—the intuitive hemisphere—in about 80 percent of their decisions.

Therefore, Taki is not alone here; many CEOs rely primarily on intuition during the processes of hiring, placing, and promoting their employees. Others say they apply it in product decisions, particularly in fashion and entertainment industries. Intuition, of course, can lead to just as many mistakes as rational logic can. By definition, creative intuition cannot be the product of a formula. But certain questions are useful in determining whether your gut feeling is worth following:

Ask yourself if you are influenced by wishful thinking and pure guesswork. Is your intuitive conclusion based on what psychologists call selective perception? Do you want to keep a

(continued)

(continued)

dying product alive simply because you have pride of authorship, or do you have some basis for your intuition? Do you want to sell off a successful product simply because it bores you? Is your conclusion due not to intuition but to mental rigidity? That is, are you reacting by habit or a desire to vindicate a past policy, refusing to recognize that a change has occurred in the environment? One of the problems encountered in the US auto and steel industries may have been that executives relied too much on their feel for the business, rather than paying attention to what their competitors around the world were doing.

Has your judgment been affected by your personal inclinations—for instance, a tendency to be either very optimistic or pessimistic? Are you allowing a flood of emotion to drown good sense? The classic case is that of the British businessperson who continued to make a money-losing product because Buckingham Palace was still buying it, even though the general public had turned thumbs down on it. The key question is the one that troubled Joan of Arc: the inner voices may be loud and clear, but do they come from heaven or hell? At the end of the day, it appears that the ultimate safeguard is to avoid stubbornness, to listen sympathetically to what others say, and to subject all decisions, whether the fruits of reason or of intuition, to searching examination.

Mortimer R. Feinberg, PhD

CHAPTER 14

Growing Anne Klein

Once Frank came on board, I worried less about spending so much time in Japan. He did a very good job not only maintaining capital but also heightening awareness of the company. Frank was exactly the man I needed for the job. In addition, the color-coordination and mix-and-match philosophy worked well together, perhaps better than I had initially anticipated.

For a few years, I let Frank run the company on his own. I would return to New York from time to time to get a status report, and I consistently saw the Anne Klein Company doing well. However, my vision had yet to materialize. After handling the mess in Japan to my satisfaction, I yearned for something new. So I started looking for apartments in New York. I wanted to spend more time at Anne Klein to guide Frank and the company in the right direction.

Although Anne Klein had been successful thus far, our growth was confined to the designer label. Those who could afford to pay top prices for our garments did, and those who could not, didn't. High-end brands are pricey and only the upper-economic crust can indulge—let alone become repeat customers. I wanted the company to branch out and cater not only to the wealthy but also to the massive—and ever-growing—middle class. The first step had been incorporating season-to-season color coordination along with mix-and-match options; however, this tactic did not change material costs. In addition, high-end brands need other kinds of emotional value as their label grows. That is, the retail prices needed to rise so the company could compete with other big names while maintaining profit margins. However, these price hikes could come only with time, and increased consumer demand must correlate with higher retail prices.

When I first moved to New York, I wanted to introduce a diffusion line, similar to what I had done in Japan with the K2 line from Takihyo's Kelly Arden line discussed in Part 1. If I could produce similar goods without sacrificing quality at a lower price point, I could attract a whole new demographic that had been previously alienated by the high prices inherent in designer brands. However, I looked into the figures and found that although I could find ways to manufacture more inexpensively, the Anne Klein brand was not yet ripe enough to introduce a lesser priced line without impeding the designer label's growth. However, the environment became much more suitable for such an introduction after a few years and steady retail price increases.

Once the Anne Klein label had a high enough price point, we could keep our current demographic buying while catering to a new one. There were, of course, inexpensive clothing lines for women; however, the most desirable styles were designer brands. With an increasingly profitable Anne Klein, I saw the potential to create a new niche in the industry: a diffusion line. These kinds of clothing lines are ubiquitous nowadays; nearly every designer label has a less expensive version of its high-end labels. However, this idea had yet to catch on during the early 1980s. Many American managers did not believe that a similar garment could be produced for a lesser price without the two lines competing with one another.

At first, everyone at the Anne Klein Company fought against my initiatives—Frank included. When I first bought into the Anne Klein Company, annual revenues were about $5 million with $800,000 net income before taxes. Five years later, revenues increased by about $2.5 million and profits too grew at the proportionate rate. Frank and many other executives argued that, "If it ain't broke, don't fix it." The

Anne Klein Company had grown, and Frank and many of his colleagues believed that the unconventional step of launching a new line could damage the current customer base. For instance, if Anne Klein was selling a dress at $500 and the diffusion line offered a similar dress at $350, why would a consumer purchase the collection line product over the diffusion line product?

In addition, the naysayers thought that the capital accumulated within the company would be eaten up and there would be little room for error should something go wrong. Frank feared that a diffusion line could turn the Anne Klein Company inside out for the following reason: because high-end designer labels cater to the wealthy, a relatively small portion of the population, the number of garments sold is limited by the demographic. However, as I explained, if Anne Klein were to bridge lower-end lines with a higher-end one, there would be interest in various demographics. This would prompt not only a jump in the number of potential customers but also a corresponding jump in material and production costs. Moreover, many of these potential customers would be turned off if we were to launch a diffusion line and not order enough materials or make enough garments. If demand outpaces supply, someone else will do the supplying. Meanwhile, the brand would be tarnished and we would have lost this avenue for growth—while perhaps inadvertently alienating some of the designer-label repeat customers.

To understand the decisions that we faced at Anne Klein at this time, it's important to have somewhat of an understanding of the hierarchy of fashion design. Many people consider high fashion to be different from what people buy on a day-to-day basis, and this is very true. Haute couture tends to stand alone as one-of-a-kind and prototypical works—made for one person and never reproduced in most cases. Big-name designers may make this kind of item, but occasionally the best designs have come from small shops that specialize only in haute couture fashion. Haute couture is the art of the fashion world. These kinds of garments are sold directly from the design studios and cater to the client's hopes, wishes, and every last desire.

One rung down from haute couture is couture, which is along the lines of bespoke fashion. The garments are semicustom, and the lines may be available only to a private clientele. Some higher-end department stores may sell these items; however, they come in limited numbers and are not finished garments upon arrival (requiring tailoring to the client). The next level down is designer-brand sportswear. The first Anne Klein label was in this category. The items are pricey but relatively available; if the public wants to purchase these garments, they're easy to find, for a price. However, it can be hard to differentiate between some designer-brand sportswear and couture. The lines are fuzzy, but designer-brand sportswear tends to reference a more approachable garment.

Next comes the bridge line. Although I will discuss this level in detail later in the chapter, this category is basically meant to raise the consumer's expectations. The quality and look of the garments here are meant to fulfill the expectations of a far more expensive garment; however, because of the cost efficiencies of mass-production and inexpensive labor, the "bridge-line" settles somewhere between designer-label fashion and affordability for the masses. Put another way, whereas a product may cost $20 in the United States, that same product may cost $5 in Malaysia or China. Many factors play into this shift in valuation for a particular item; these elements range from currency spreads and different standards of living to reduced cost of shipment (if the good may be manufactured in that country, applicable duties, and quality control standards). The bridge line terminology comes from the fact that mass manufacturing garments in the Far East with European fabrics *bridged* the qualities of couture or designer-brand sportswear lines with the more inexpensive lines. The scale of manufacturing also offered improvements in quality and consistency, as all garments are made the same way rather than one piece at a time.

The lines at the bottom of the totem pole are the better line, moderate line, and budget line—in that order. The better lines are manufactured like bridge lines, but with less expensive (lower-quality) fabrics and are sold as inexpensive options at department stores. The moderate and budget lines, however, are sold exclusively at chain stores. These are the least expensive and tend to combine the cheapest fabrics with the lowest production costs. These goods have a customer base in chain stores, whose customers search for economy over quality and fashion. Of course, even the low-end lines attempt to follow trends, but consumers who are the most interested in the latest fashions will probably not be buying from these lines. The bridge lines are trendy; the better, moderate, and budget lines offer garments a year or two behind. The design room for the three most inexpensive lines is much smaller (or nonexistent) compared with those of the bridge lines and above, and the choice of fabrics tends to be much smaller. With some recent notable exceptions—such as a Target line designed by famous brand-name designer Isaac Mizrahi and Vera Wang's Simply Vera line for Kohl's—talented and renowned designers have shied away from these lesser lines due to significant fiscal constraints and subpar quality. Therefore, my experience building the Anne Klein Company's first bridge line, and the first true bridge-line in the United States, was certainly a challenge.

Building a bridge line was a painstaking process, with little room for error. Although the rewards appeared to trump the risks, this new line also necessitated certain price increases on the designer-label side; this was so the bridge line would be recognized as a less-expensive yet still high-quality garment. Once the margins were large enough on the designer-label end, we could create a more affordable—although not cheap—bridge line to offer a larger demographic better fashion options.

The reasons a designer label can charge higher price points has to do with the quality of materials and the difficulty of the manufacturing processes. For example, a dress or suit that requires single-stitch hand finishing will have added labor costs. Many higher-end designer skirts have fewer rather than more seams. These skirts tend to have cleaner lines and are made from better fabrics. However, if we were to change the manufacturing process and the materials, prices could be slashed further—and we could maintain a healthy profit margin. It's become increasingly common nowadays to change from the high-end fabrics in the collection line to another, less expensive fabric for the bridge line. It's difficult for the average consumer to tell the difference between the myriad wools and cashmere. Pashmina, for example, can be bought inexpensively; yet this wool—which is gathered from the underhair of northern Indian goats—shares some of the same characteristics in color and feel with cashmere blends.

After some careful thought, we knew that it would be only a matter of time before we could launch the new line. From an accounting perspective, my initial position in Anne Klein came through the Takihyo Company Ltd. in Japan. I owned majority equity in the Takihyo Company, which meant that I had indirect ownership of Anne Klein.

However, I started a new US-based entity to hold the Anne Klein Company, and I planned to buy that entity from Takihyo. At the time, Takihyo was experiencing the worst the 1970s had to offer. I therefore wanted to find a way to make a bit more money for Takihyo while keeping my buyout price low enough that I, too, could profit from the transaction down the line.

Just before we were considering launching the bridge line, I arranged for Takihyo Inc.—a US corporation—to conduct a leveraged buyout for Anne Klein from Takihyo Company Ltd. At the time, the first oil shock, the Nixon crises, and the subsequent energy crisis had damaged Takihyo Company Ltd.'s bottom line. I wanted to find a way to help the organization out while also strengthening my position of control at Anne Klein and allowing me to manage the company on my own. The accountants at Takihyo Company Ltd. priced the Anne Klein Company at about $12 million based on its earnings power. I knew that I could take control while offering yearly installments if I were to pay for Anne Klein over a period of 10 years through a leveraged buyout.

The first determinant of a company's health, according to the stock market, is usually its price-to-earnings ratio. This figure tends to be a lot higher in a well-known, growing company than in what some would call a value company, or one with a low price-to-earnings ratio. However, as a manager, there seems to be only three ways to value a company: asset base, earnings, and potential growth value. Financiers always argue which one trumps the others, whereas the better money managers are inclined to take an integrated approach.

However, because I wanted Takihyo Company Ltd. to benefit from the sale—and because the Anne Klein Company had virtually no asset base—I took earnings (which was about $2 million at the time) and multiplied that six times. Twelve million dollar was closer to what Takihyo Company Ltd. offered to pay, but I believed the growth value for the company outweighed current earnings power. I estimated the value of the company, as a result, closer to $20 million. The growth rate for the Anne Klein collection line was tremendous; adding a new bridge line could provide far more value than the conservative 6 or even 12 times current earnings calculation. Because Anne Klein was privately owned, all of the income came in after everyone—including myself—had been paid out. Moreover, because the company was making a couple million dollars a year, and Takihyo Inc. was also benefiting, I could afford to pay $20 million in total for the company for full control and Takihyo Company Ltd. would have made a considerable gain in its initial investment five years earlier. In my opinion, the $20 million figure was still working in my favor.

After waiting a couple of years and watching the profit margins grow by leaps and bounds for the Anne Klein collection line, the bridge line made much more fiscal sense. The Anne Klein Company was building a significant cash reserve, but there was not enough to fulfill the capital requirements of the bridge line, Anne Klein II. However, the market seemed to yearn for this bridge line, and we wanted to find a way to make it happen.

The bottom-line growth at the Anne Klein Company gave us enhanced access to capital and additional sources of credit. Because we wanted to expand operations and were doing very well, I knew we would have our choice of banks and other lenders. Starting the bridge line required more capital than what we could pay while maintaining the collection line. However, I chose to leverage our current reserves to expand the company.

Although materials and manufacturing are expensive, the cost basis for the Anne Klein collection was far less than for the bridge line. However, the latter offered more value as the lower price point would allow us to sell in greater volumes. As mentioned previously, the collection lines cater only to the small number of women who can afford to pay those pieces. The bridge line, however, would cater to a larger audience—I calculated that the new line would cost about four times more to manufacture, distribute, and market than the collection.

Once we had quelled the arguments over the massive capital commitment required to launch a bridge line, we started discussing different names in the boardroom. There were so many different possibilities that we didn't know where to begin. But because everyone at the company was already calling it "Anne Klein 2," the name stuck. Of course, we could have changed the name to something fresh and new, but the name seemed to work. Instead of the Arabic numeral 2, we decided to use Roman numerals. At the time, there were so many other companies that were using numbers in their branding, we thought the Roman numerals would have a more lasting impact on consumers. I also liked how the "two" in Anne Klein II could represent a supplement to the collection. I wanted the two lines to have that link so that an Anne Klein collection customer could consider buying from both lines to mix-and-match or coordinate for a less formal look. From these blueprints came America's first true bridge line, which is now dubbed "sportswear." The line would change not only the profitability of fashion houses but also how Americans thought about fashion. For the first time, beautiful, name-brand clothing was within reach of the country's largest consumer demographic. First, however, we needed additional capital.

Going Against the Grain

When you introduce subordinates to a new project—as Tomio did with his bridge-line concept—you are talking about change. Change has both positive and negative implications. On the one hand, change offers us the freedom for new possibilities. On the other hand, change can equate with fear, as we saw in the previous chapter. To win the fullest enthusiasm and cooperation possible from your staff, you must therefore maximize the positive stimulation and minimize the threat.

There are three things a manager must convey in this situation: personal enthusiasm, effective communication, and selective job structuring. You must first of all radiate your own enthusiasm and confidence that the job will get done—and get done well. Unfortunately, management enthusiasm, to a great degree, has gone out of style. In 1925, Sinclair Lewis made *babbitry* an ignominious household word—and an entire breed of scientific managers grew up feeling that it was babbitry to show too much enthusiasm for the job or for some particular aspect of it. Such enthusiasm was identified with simple-minded pep talks and naive optimism.

However, more recent observation indicates that we have gone much too far in dispelling enthusiasm from the executive suite. Today's average worker is not going to display much zest for his or her job—at least overtly. Workers who do are viewed suspiciously by colleagues; others think there is something odd about them. Nevertheless, many people like their jobs—or at least they want to like them. So they look to their managers for cues. If the boss conducts himself or herself like a dispassionate robot, then his or her employees are likely to conclude that perhaps there really is something wrong with getting all revved up or that the job is not something that should excite them at all. It is therefore up to the manager to provide a cue for enthusiasm in a useful and systematic fashion.

The executive's job is to strike a balance between winning active cooperation and maintaining control of the situation. Six general guidelines can help one accomplish this task. First, the manager should disseminate full information about the new project or assignment. Without endangering security, it's best to risk giving out too much information rather than too little. Second, the manager should show how the project ties in with the organization's overall goals and health. When people know only about their finite, limited departmental goals, they are working in a vacuum. Take, for example, the situation in which the manager of an accounting department tries to get his people to speed up certain transactions. Experience tells us that he will succeed in doing so if he emphasizes how this accelerated process will affect sales, production, customer relations, and so forth—the company's other major, and sometimes more glamorous, undertakings.

Third, the manager must talk to each key subordinate about his or her particular role in this new responsibility. Depending on the individual, the manager may give more or less leeway to the employee to structure him or her; however, it's also necessary to make sure the employee has a structure that he or she understands. Fourth, the manager needs to manifest his or her own enthusiasm. Managers should make it clear that they believe the overall objective is demanding and worthy but that they have every confidence in the department's ability to meet it. Fifth,

(continued)

(continued)

the manager should establish short-term goals for each individual that can be reached fairly quickly and that are easily seen. Last, the manager should increase interaction with subordinates while a new project is getting under way. The manager should talk to people. The goal is to find out what problems they are facing and help them solve those problems. The manager should pat employees on the back for accomplishments. It should be clear to everyone that the manager is involved and doing his or her share.

Mortimer R. Feinberg, PhD

CHAPTER 15

No Kickbacks

With limited capital for such a massive operation, before approaching banks and lenders, the new Anne Klein II division needed an agent. Although I had an extensive network in the Far East, I could not oversee everything and we weren't ready to get involved without the bridge line in production and selling in stores. For Anne Klein II to become successful, we needed the right production and manufacturers as well as proper quality control. We opened a small office in Hong Kong, but we preferred to spend less capital on labor than future distribution and production costs. Because of our budget for the launch of the line, however, we held a number of concerns. First and foremost would be the loss of control.

In Hong Kong, where we would do most of our manufacturing for Anne Klein II, there was a practice of giving incorrect yields for particular garments to distributors and wholesalers. More particularly, a manufacturer might need 2.5 yards to complete a dress, but the manufacturer would quote us at 3.1 yards. Although 0.6 yards may not be enough to make one dress, when buying many rolls of fabric and sending it to Hong Kong for manufacturing, that extra 0.6 yards per dress can add up. Many manufacturers would take that 0.6 yards and make another or similar dress for sale in wholesale or retail markets. Since many of our fabrics were unique, Anne Klein II couldn't afford to let something like this happen. For this reason, we paid more to warehouse the unused textiles and held the Hong Kong office to supervise the manufacturing. Since our lines were coordinated across seasons, I reasoned it would not be too difficult to come up with uses for the unused materials.

Regardless, we needed help to launch Anne Klein II. We found and hired a contractor called Cambridge to manufacture Anne Klein II. At the time, Cambridge was under the Swire and Maclaine corporate umbrella, now called the Swire Group (Swire). Swire was and remains to this day a massive company spread across the Far East and Oceania. At first, I was unaware of Cambridge's association until meeting with Lydia Dunne, leader of the subdivision. Lydia's group was to work closely in correspondence with our Hong Kong office and our production manager in New York, Dan Homesly.

During our contract negotiations with Cambridge, I had mentioned the need for a letter of credit to purchase textiles from Italy for the bridge line. Anne Klein had a letter of credit from the banks in the United States, but we would need international financial support. Although Anne Klein was growing, we hadn't touched all four corners of the globe. Swire, however, had. The majority equity holder in Cathay Pacific Airways and various other public companies, Swire had access to substantial capital. Lydia mentioned that Swire could act as financier for a part of the project to secure fabrics from Italy. Cambridge was also an evidence shipper and manufacturer.

To ship goods, one needs a quota allowance. Since we were manufacturing in Hong Kong and shipping to the United States, one of our cost concerns was this quota. The United States is infamous for taxing or disallowing the distribution of certain imported goods. Sometimes if unfulfilled quota allowances existed, an agent could sell the credits to another company. There are trading companies in the Far East that only buy and sell marked-up quotas for manufacturers. Evidence shippers like Cambridge can earn quotas. Because Cambridge had a factory and a shipping business, we had less cause for concern. After handling these logistics, all we had to do was wait for the line to hit the stores and pray my instincts were right.

And they were; we did much better than we anticipated. Anne Klein II was an instant success. We maintained the integrity of our collection line by timing the introduction properly, and we created the first large-scale bridge line catering to a new price-point for the American markets. The line required a new infrastructure. Although we wanted to oversee everything, we could not handle all the responsibility with our existing staff. We hired new personnel, creating a new division within the company.

Everything seemed to be going great until I received an odd phone call at Takihyo Inc. from Shorty Chow at Cambridge. Chow proposed putting some funds aside from the current pricing structure of production as if we were in the loop of whatever had been going on overseas. We didn't know what to make of it. At the time, Frank Mori was in the United States and I was abroad, but I flew back immediately to initiate a conversation to solve the problem. We feared something was going on behind our backs. At the time, rebates were commonplace in Hong Kong, and no one was there to police or control these kinds of matters. We would be a laughingstock if we mentioned this issue to Chinese officials at the time since kickbacks were a part of nearly every business. To get to the bottom of this, we would have to dig.

The first place we looked had been our price quotes for production, and we cross-checked them with some of the other figures Chow could provide. We found that while Anne Klein may have been paying $10 and we were billed for that amount, the real cost of production may have been $8. That remaining $2 was sent somewhere else. Where, how much, and for how long, we had no idea, but we had identified the problem. Frank and I set up a meeting first with Lydia from Cambridge to go over our findings.

We hired Cambridge to handle some of our operations because it was a subsidiary of Swire and Maclaine. It owned public companies, such as Cathay Pacific Airways. We thought because Cambridge was within this massive corporate structure, little corruption could occur. We were dead wrong. I told Lydia frankly, "If someone is receiving rebates against the best interests of my company, I want to know the truth." Lydia reacted with a similar response. The lines started to blur as to whom we could and could not trust.

We had a team of accountants dig through all money paid and received and compared those numbers to the price quotes offered to

Anne Klein in the United States. They found money was moving in different directions. Making matters worse, although Lydia gave no direct confession, she may have been a player in the kickback operation. We found one of her employees, Gracie Fore, had been taking kickbacks as well. I mention Gracie here because a couple years after starting at Anne Klein, Gracie had married our production manager, Dan Homesly. The most disappointing element of this was that our own production manager was stealing from our company. Dan should have told us the manufacturers in Hong Kong could offer us a lesser price on production rather than pocket the difference and be dishonest about the numbers. Dan and Gracie were putting the corporation's money into their own pockets.

Frank and I confronted Dan and Gracie. What they had done was wrong, and we asked they return what was owed. There was some resistance, but they knew what they had done was wrong and returned the money. I fired Dan for insubordination and found a replacement for the production manager. Afterward, I went to Cambridge and called Lydia out on her dishonesty and lack of integrity. Lydia thought she had Anne Klein wrapped around her finger because it was handling the overseas production. She responded, "If you don't trust us and don't want to do business with us, leave." Frank and Larry Stern, our chief financial officer, didn't know what to do. They didn't like what had happened, but we had due dates for our production that we had to meet. They suggested we delay severing the relationship with Cambridge until our contract expired. This option would have allowed us to keep the same production schedule without any bumps in the road, but we would be giving those who stole from us more business and another chance to steal. Although Frank and Larry thought ending the relationship with Cambridge would be a bad idea for the Anne Klein Company, I refused to continue working with them. Against Frank and Larry's advice, I terminated the relationship with Cambridge and hired Doris To full-time to fulfill Cambridge's functions in the Far East.

Doris had been an office manager for the small Anne Klein operation in Hong Kong. This office specialized in quality control, and consequently, Doris had all the staff and knowledge necessary to oversee production quality control and shipping. I knew she was a hard worker and would have Anne Klein's best interests at heart. Frank and

Larry thought she could not get the job done in time, but I believed in her and I introduced her to some of my contacts in Hong Kong to expedite matters. An old family friend, Christopher Cheng, current CEO and Chairman of Wing-Tie, and Benson Tong, Chairman of Tong Textiles, supplied the new office with a chief operating officer and chief financial officer to help Doris. Only with the strong relationships I had fostered over the years in Hong Kong could I have terminated the Cambridge contract, knowing we could figure it out. The business was transferred out of the hands of Cambridge and into Doris's hands. With all of Doris's hard work, she wound up saving the Anne Klein Company time in the production process and money.

Managing Crisis

Tomio chose to terminate a contract against the suggestions of his business partner and legal counsel because he was aware of other means to get the job done. In this particular case, he successfully managed disaster. The landscape was dark and muddy. However, with some legwork, Tomio uncovered the truth and made his plan of action. The first ground rule in these situations is to avoid making hasty and ill-informed decisions. Don't start with a black-and-white imperative; form an opinion from various sources, and concoct a solution. Observing a situation and avoiding panic is the cleanest and most effective means to move into a crisis situation. Tomio started with his fellow executives in Anne Klein and opened a discussion with Lydia Dunne at Cambridge before making any accusations or terminating the company's contract. He had the accountants do the forensic work, and he started conversations about how to solve the problem if everything turned sour, which, as he learned, it did.

Next, it is important to distinguish between unusual situations and those needing your immediate attention, as opposed to those that may appear unpleasant but are not critical. Because

(continued)

(continued)

some discussion exists among some employees may reflect a personal difficulty and not a widespread problem. Once you've diagnosed the problem, ask yourself if it will get better with the passage of time.

When disaster looms, it sometimes seems as if everything is coming apart at once. Dan Homesly and Gracie Fore were big surprises, but there was only one key element: the inherent hubris in believing that you never get caught with your hand in the cookie jar. Recognizing this hubris, Tomio could concentrate his initial thinking on the critical factors to solve the problem. He found alternative solutions to Cambridge to solve his production crisis.

Mortimer R. Feinberg, PhD

CHAPTER 16

Elevating the Designer

Long before the launch of Anne Klein II, Donna, the head designer at Anne Klein, desired to individuate and start her own brand. At first, she wanted a new line under the Anne Klein umbrella. She was the only one who thought starting a new line with her name within Anne Klein was a good idea. Frank and I believed the Anne Klein Collection as well as the new bridge line had a distinctive look. Donna wanted to do something unique. Any innovation within the Anne Klein brand image, we believed, would clash. Keeping any new project differentiated from the parent was critical. So, Donna and I started talking about forming a new company.

Donna, however, was apprehensive. Starting a new line with her own design risked creating a new brand and business. Also, the fear of failure after such a long run at the Anne Klein Company haunted her dreams. Understandably, Donna had never made a name for herself since she had been working under the protection of an established brand. Donna noted her fears. I stepped back and let her continue working as she had in the Anne Klein design room. Anne Klein was doing so well, I didn't want to lose the conceptual strength behind the name.

However, after 10 years, I feared Donna was talking too much with other members in the company about her future dreams. Her ambivalence marked a weakness in the design room that neither I nor other key executives could continue to tolerate. I knew that if Donna were to blow hot and cold for much longer, the morale at the Anne Klein Company could dwindle. I believed her good friend and co-designer at the Anne Klein Company, Louis Dell'Olio, was strong enough to handle the challenges of a collection alone.

After launching Anne Klein II, I knew our arrangement with Donna would have to be short-lived. If I didn't do something, I could lose her to someone else willing to take the necessary risks. One Friday afternoon, Frank and I called Donna into my office. At the time, my office was on a different floor from the designers in the same building. We met in the conference room, and I asked her how she was doing. She still showed the same apprehension and ambivalence as in prior encounters. Donna didn't want to leave Anne Klein because she had reached a level of comfort. I, however, thought there was much potential waiting to be unleashed. Frank and I knew she wouldn't make a decision on her own. We didn't want her to have any choice in the matter. I fired her and directed her to report Monday morning to the conference room on the fourth floor of 205 West 39th Street.

Firing Donna and starting a new partnership between Takihyo Inc. and her would require a lot of capital, patience, and ingenuity. We knew we had mountains to climb. Before I acquired the Anne Klein Company, Gunther Oppenheim and Anne Klein had done most of the heavy lifting. They had done a good job of launching the line and activating public attention. Although the company wasn't growing as quickly as it had under Takihyo's watch, the hard part was done. Anne's name was gaining recognition and respect within the industry.

Donna, on the other hand, was not a household name. All of the Anne Klein ads had Donna's and Louis's name, so some branding existed, but the "Anne Klein" name was on an entirely different plane. However, we had to start from scratch. I had to recruit the right people to help with the new venture. In the first days working together on the branding, Donna and I browsed through a number of different magazines to brainstorm how to establish our new image. We found a number of great ads, but one caught our eye. The credit read Peter Arnell. He would have to be the one to brand our company for the public eye. Peter's creativity and ingenuity outmatched most of the other ads. I called him and set up a first meeting.

In our first meeting, I asked Peter to create some images for the company that could work. I wanted three images: corporate, brand name, and product. Each needed a distinctive feeling and message. In the corporate image, I did not want faces, styles, garments, or the color of the seasons. Donna and I wanted to make a point that we were an American company and, more specifically, a company berthed in New York. We named the new company Donna Karan New York, and our corporate image would need to fit with our name. When incorporating seasonality into a company's image, a brand can be frozen in time; I wanted the corporate image to be beyond time.

The brand image centered on our products. We could not limit ourselves to garments, as we would at some point get into accessories as well as menswear and other lines. Our product at the beginning had been a classic, chic, and sophisticated line for international jet-setting women, but we wanted to keep the door open for other opportunities. The image would have to be all-inclusive for whatever avenue our future growth would take.

Lastly, the product image would express the flavor of the season with individual items ranging from shoes and belts to garments and more. This is the most ephemeral type of branding for us. We wanted to send a message about a particular product to the public. These images were meant for advertisements and banners, and they were produced on a schedule in line with the development of each new line.

In truth, I was somewhat unfair to Peter. Since the Donna Karan Collection had no collection as of yet, we had nothing to show. We were starting from scratch, so Peter had no idea what direction he should follow: he was on his own for this one. However, I trusted his aesthetic. The only other hints I gave him were the following: The consumers for this line have a sophisticated and chic yet classic air. Our brand should fit with jet-setters, international businesswomen with a high level of taste. They are conservative but fashion conscious.

Before Peter's creation of the image of Donna Karan New York, no one had ever used photographs without models to brand a fashion house.

Although Peter has caught some flak in the press for being difficult to his employees, his brilliance has remained unmatched. I knew Peter could come up with a design that would fit our needs. Peter returned to us with a black-and-white, blurred photo of the Brooklyn Bridge. When Donna and I saw this image, we were speechless. Peter's photo was so strong, Donna had tears in her eyes.

We called the first line the Donna Karan New York Collection. Peter's design was perfect. The typeface was thin, in a contemporary-looking matte gold on the black-and-white photograph—timelessly New York, yet bold and provocative. The design fit seamlessly, building a directed sense of emotional value into the brand.

Other than our work with Peter, we focused on hiring a full-time staff. I let Donna handle the design team and I would fill the business side. At first, we wanted to find people in the business whom we knew would be interested. Though I have relied on headhunters many other times to bring the right candidates, I had few people whom I could trust to do the job right. Because this project was so new, it was more fragile and needed careful hands to make our dream a reality. We had a hard time finding the right production manager. A few other people came in to do the job, but no one made sense. Steve Weiss, Donna's husband, had pitched in his time alongside of other production staff to fill the void. It was difficult to find the right person to be our production manager, so we did our best with the staff we had and Steve's help for some time.

At first, however, revenues did not compare to initial capital contributions. Frank, who was the first against creating Donna Karan New York, argued that taking money away from Takihyo meant losing some of the asset basis available for the two of us. A week before firing Donna to have her in the design room as Takihyo's partner in the Donna Karan New York office, Frank and I had dinner at the Le Parker Meridien Hotel in midtown Manhattan. Frank was nearly in tears fearing the death of all of his hard work. He wanted nothing to do with it. Being the majority equity holder of the company, however, I had final vote and veto power. I told Frank this was how I wanted to run the business. This was how I saw an increase in our bottom line. Moreover, since he held a small stake in Takihyo Inc., I did not assign him any responsibility but offered 10 percent equity since he was my partner.

I understood his concern, but I believed in Donna's ability. She had brought the Anne Klein Company from a small revenue producer to the first sportswear company offering clothing to the masses. As an intangible asset, I knew this new venture could materialize profits far greater than what we could amass at the Anne Klein Company. I continued, however, to face considerable resistance. Everyone from accountants and lawyers to those closest to me advised Donna Karan New York was chasing bad money with good. When we made an original agreement with Donna Karan New York, Takihyo was only committed to contribute $3 million. However, within the first three years, we spent roughly $16 million to create the brand and have enough working capital. Despite their cries that I would go broke and take Anne Klein down with me, I stuck to my conviction.

The company's future rested on Donna's first solo collection. As mentioned previously, collection lines tend to be expensive and only the wealthiest demographics show interest; that is, consumers who spend hundreds or even thousands on a dress without batting an eye. Arnell's creative genius teed up the collection as a line to be had, using attractive advertisements to heighten Donna's name and to create a strong, bold image for the brand. I learned early on that without brand creation, a terrific collection line will fail. Without a terrific line, branding only takes the lines so far. Some designers might gain momentary fame after releasing an effective advertising and marketing campaign, but when the product fails to meet expectations, so too does the company.

Arnell's brilliant advertisements fit well with Donna's fashion aesthetic, launching the first line into the stratosphere. Advertisements only go so far, but publicity goes much farther: Donna's first solo collection line was a hit and was featured on the front page of nearly every major newspaper worldwide. Donna's collection created a dramatically new, fresh look. Robert Lee Morris contributed to Donna's new look with a complementary line of accessories they both designed. The first line debuted at our brand new showroom at 550 Seventh Avenue for the press and special guests. After the show, the guests of the vernissage gave a standing ovation.

Managing Creative People

What we have said about getting people interested applies to a great majority of those who report to you. These are the average, near-average, little-better-than-average performers who, let's face it, constitute the backbone of most departments and most companies. No troupe is made up completely of stars. If you are able to "turn on" the people of reasonable competency who work for you, you will be accomplishing one of the fundamental tasks of management.

However, every operation contains, or should contain, exceptional performers (those creative people, often with oddball traits), such as Donna Karan in the previous chapter. These types tend to provide the most dramatic solutions to the biggest problems. Some managers are frightened of these types. They don't understand them or they can't handle them. Tomio recognized his fear that Donna might leave if a new opportunity were to arise, so he acted on this impulse. His judgment led him to an understanding of what I'd call the "creative exception." For most operations to rise to great heights, these "creative exceptions" are crucial. You should want to rise to the heights, at least once in a while. It is exhilarating, and it is sometimes just plain necessary.

Sometimes, however, you have to tell these types to require what they want. Sometimes, people want (meaning, need) to be told what to do. "Free rein" for subordinates can be good but can be unrealistic at every juncture as Tomio pointed out in the previous chapter. Conventional management wisdom dictates that the boss should talk things out, listen to everybody's ideas, and let people participate in working toward solutions to problems. But the gifted manager pays the price. The late, towering management thinker Abraham Maslow pointed out, "For one thing, the superior person is apt to get extremely restless in such a situation, and the strain upon his body is apt to be much greater because of the necessity for controlling himself and inhibiting his impulses. He may easily and quickly see the truth that all the others are struggling toward very slowly, and keeping his mouth shut can be physical torture."

Phony egalitarianism makes it tough for subordinates as well. They know the boss is likely to reach the finish line before they are halfway around the track. So, what happens? "They are less apt to work hard because the work is useless and senseless. Why should they sweat for three days to work toward a solution of a particular problem when they know all the time that the superior one can see the solution in three minutes? The tendency, therefore, is for all the others to become passive. By contrast, they feel that they are less capable than they actually are, and more stupid, too."

So don't listen to those who say, "Don't take yourself too seriously. You're a peacock today and a feather-duster tomorrow." You are a manager. Unless you are burdened with an extraordinarily weak ego, you must admit to yourself you are the superior. Tomio took control of the situation with Donna to create a company and brand that would far surpass his first endeavor with the Anne Klein Company because he was willing to take the opinions of others with a grain of salt when he saw more opportunity on the horizon.

Mortimer R. Feinberg, PhD

CHAPTER 17

DKNY—A New Brand,
a Diffusion Line

The first seven easy pieces comprising the Donna Karan New York collection line debuted in 1985. Donna and I knew the company was heading in the right direction, but it was hard to convince others when the bottom line seemed to sink deeper into the red. All of my peers thought the company would go broke, and I would lose everything I had earned at the Anne Klein Company. Accountants, lawyers, and many businesspersons struggled to find proper valuations for the many intangibles on the company's balance sheet. Donna's talent was perhaps the most nebulous of all. After two and half years of bleeding, Donna Karan New York reached a precipice: Revenues were on track to grow larger than operating expenses, and we would reach the black. However, much like the Anne Klein Collection, Donna Karan New York was catering to a wealthy demographic, and we needed to branch out to increase our top and bottom lines.

The concept of the bridge line as we applied it at the Anne Klein Company didn't seem to fit with Donna's new design. A diffusion line is quite different from a bridge line. Diffusion lines do not necessarily offer similar products at different price points and, thus, different manufacturing processes and fabrics. On the other hand, a diffusion line functions as a proxy to the original line, a kind of extension into another area of one's lifestyle. The Donna Karan diffusion line was started to offer the same consumers a new spin and a broader line of goods, which consequently had a much wider price range. Discussing the emergence of this concept into a reality begins with a bit more information on the growth of the Donna Karan Company as well as a deeper comparison between Anne Klein II and the concepts pre-mising DKNY.

The inaugurating seasons of Donna Karan New York offered a new look with a classic flair. Donna created a fantastic line with focus. This direction gave the Donna Karan New York corporate image some room to breathe. As management, we could step back and take a look at where the opportunity would be for us. Donna and I used Anne Klein II as a launching pad for new ideas. The timing for Anne Klein II was perfect. The market conditions could not have been bet-ter. The perception of the Anne Klein II brand was aligned with the collection line nearly at half the price. Of course, major concessions were made to meet that criteria regarding materials and manufac-turing methods, but the look was the same between the parent and diffusion lines.

Donna and I knew we couldn't re-create a less expensive Donna Karan New York. Anne Klein had a long history of providing the working, metropolitan women of the world with business attire. Long before I partnered with Anne and Chip Rubenstein, Anne Klein began to amass a following. Donna Karan New York, however, was new. The image we created had its own space in the fashion world and re-creating a line of only seven pieces at a lower price point could lead to more trouble than we could have bargained for. Unlike Anne Klein II, a less expensive Donna Karan New York line would confuse the brand's image. However, because the collection was so focused, we saw opportunity in creating another brand with a different public persona. Other than death and taxes, the only other certainty in life is that women want to look beautiful, confident, and sophisticated, but no one wants to be dressed up all of the time.

From this view came the concept for a secondary diffusion line. We wanted to create a new brand and line geared to a similar con-sumer but with a more casual approach. The Donna Karan New York collection is meant to be comfortable but not meant to be worn on the weekends, on vacation, or at home. We reasoned if there were a more casual line with a nexus in the design room, we could capture a far larger market and diversify the company with a new brand of products.

We went back to Peter Arnell to discuss the concept for the new line. We wanted to continue focusing on New York as the center of our image, but we wanted to capture the city from a much different angle. The secondary brand needed to be institutional. I learned that at Anne Klein, when Anne died, the brand name was negatively affected. It was difficult publicizing someone's name who was no longer alive, and the challenge emerged again when creating Anne Klein II. Branding a person's name eternally requires a lot of time, money, and energy. I was more interested in a brand that wasn't Donna's name but had some proximity to the collection.

Peter came up with the name, some revolutionary design concepts for our advertisements, and some additional accessories.[1] The first logo Peter created was in bold, black capital letters in stark contrast to Donna Karan New York's femininity. However, the font was too strong, with too much contrast. We asked him to come up with a solution.

He responded by placing an aerial shot of the Statue of Liberty with Manhattan in the background within the text DKNY on a black background. Other than merely addressing the overwhelming nature of the thickness of the logo's font, this approach provided consistency with the image we wanted to promote. This particular photo manipulation was painted on the side of a building on West Houston Street in New York City to welcome passersby into one of the city's largest shopping areas, SoHo. This advertisement boosted Arnell's fame as an advertiser as it was the first of its kind. The ad remained on the building for nearly 20 years.

In this period, Donna Karan became a household name. All the money we had spent to start the company paid off in brand recognition. From then on, we had a more marketable brand. This advantage made selling merchandise easier with the big department stores and

---

[1]Peter designed buttons to look like New York City manhole covers and he designed fire hydrants as belt buckles and clasps.

gave us an edge over our competition. In one of the earlier chapters, I wrote about my basketball coach, Mr. Taketomi. With Anne Klein II and Donna Karan, I took his words of wisdom to heart and believed in my conviction. Taketomi stated the three most important elements to being successful reside in good preparation, knowing the competition, and realizing you have little room for negativity once the first two have been taken into account. Spending the extra effort to reconsider how to approach a diffusion line with Anne Klein II and DKNY gave both ventures a considerable moat around the businesses.

Anne Klein II offered a wider demographic, a palatable design concept at an affordable price while maintaining the original collection through slight modifications of the lines and dramatic price differentials. Although DKNY was geared to a similar demographic, other socioeconomic classes took part in our sales because the concept and perception had changed. Instead of the eveningwear promoted in the collection line, DKNY was more casual, opening the door to new design fronts as well as a lower price point due to the nature of materials used and manufacturing processes. A more casual jacket should be less expensive than a formal one. However, these two ventures came with a mixed blessing.

Although Anne Klein II was successful at first, with some time the company and its brands lost their edge. There was a considerable movement toward a polarity in fashion between high-end designer collections and casual wear. More people wanted to dress one way or the other, and the Anne Klein image started to fade as new fashion trends emerged. Perhaps the consumer has always been fickle. If something goes out of style, revenues can be slammed as a result. If a celebrity says something is out, the brand image and business suffer. Moreover, Anne Klein was no longer minting money the way it had been after I took Donna out of the design room.

At first, everything was fine at Anne Klein, but that was because a number of seasons had been designed in advance with Donna's oversight. After those few seasons, Louis Dell'Olio had full control. With his first seasons as the chief designer, the product had changed, with less direction and more confusion. Other than a change in market conditions, Anne Klein and Anne Klein II became less attractive to the mainstream. We fired Louis Dell'Olio and hired one designer after another. None of them were up to snuff. Finding another

Donna was proving difficult. Shortly thereafter, we learned of Arthur Levine, who used to work for us at Takihyo, Inc. and owned a firm called Kaspar.

Arthur understood we were having trouble and was interested in taking on the challenge of revamping the collection and the diffusion line. He believed in the company and wanted a well-known company under Kaspar's umbrella. I had been so preoccupied with Donna Karan New York and DKNY that I couldn't offer Anne Klein the much needed attention. Additionally, since revenues had started to decline, it seemed like the right time to exit. After a series of conversations and negotiations, Takihyo sold Anne Klein to Kaspar. Unfortunately, Kaspar could not continue holding for too long. Arthur was unable to turn the line around and soon resold the business to the publicly traded Jones Apparel New York. While Frank and I left with golden parachutes from the Anne Klein sale, it was unfortunate the brand couldn't be resuscitated.

At Donna Karan New York, we had a series of challenges. When we started the business, the company was only Donna and me. We had to build the executive team from the bottom up. We put some Anne Klein employees temporarily into executive positions. Not until Donna and I found Steve Ruzo through a headhunter did we have a president for the company. Though we would have preferred to find someone within the existing circle, Ruzo was a natural match. He got along with Donna and Donna liked him. Since the operational executive and the designer would have to communicate frequently, getting along was essential to the company's future or at least Ruzo's future with the company.

Unlike the Anne Klein II line, DKNY was a wider reaching vision. Anne Klein II catered to office-wear for women. DKNY catered to men, women, and eventually children, filling the gap between office-casual wear and at-home clothing. The possibilities within this perception shift were larger than our previous incarnation. Additionally, new issues arose at the workplace: Steve Weiss, Donna's new husband, wanted more responsibility at the company. With so much money coming into the company, Donna justified placing him in an executive position. Steve had been in and out of our corporate offices. He was an artist and didn't have a full-time position anywhere, and Donna had him stick around because he convinced her he could help out. From time to time, we needed his assistance as well. Free help is something hard to back away from. Somewhere along the line Donna gave or sold Steve Weiss 10 percent of her share of the company. At that point, Donna Karan had become a household name, and the image didn't seem to be fading. Donna may have justified he could do little to damage the company considering the increasing revenues and profit margins. However, Steve's equity position sullied any chance for us as management to engage in direct and transparent communication. Because Steve was Donna's husband, either party could use the other to play both sides of the equation. With a subtle form of manipulation, the Donna-said-Steve-said game emerged as a point of frequent conversation. Needless to say, I became worried.

At times, Donna would come to me with certain questions or ask direct subordinates to do certain tasks that Steve Ruzo or I believed not to be in the company's best interest. Steve Weiss would do the same when Donna wasn't around. In both cases, the interlocutors brought an issue to the table that supposedly wasn't their own. Exacerbating matters, Donna and I trusted each other when we started the company. Neither she nor I saw any reason to set up the partnership any differently than split down the center. I would offer her capital and executive oversight while she was running the design room. When the company started to grow, and DKNY became a household name, everything changed. Donna had as much say as I did in the boardroom. If we disagreed, Donna still had the authority and the right to fulfill her own or Steve's desires. In either case, we could do little to nothing to stop her.

These disagreements brought the end of my half ownership of the Donna Karan Company. Before Donna gave or sold her husband an equity position, Steve Weiss was an aspiring painter and a sculptor. I do not know his other credentials; I only knew that Donna loved him. Since I trusted Donna and had worked with her for years, I never thought things would become so complicated. The first disagreement arose with the launch of the company's first fragrance.

Donna and Steve must have talked about it at length. Other designers were releasing fragrance lines, but Donna Karan New York did not have one. The beauty of the perfume business is the link between the price and brand image. If a company has a strong brand image, the product will do well provided the company did not bottle skunk spray. Since fragrances are made with little scent solute and a lot of solvent, mostly alcohol, the material cost of the perfume is little, leaving high profit margins. The primary cost of the product is not the perfume but the bottles in which it is sold. Research and development costs occur, but with a fragrance marketed to a large consumer base, those figures disappear off the balance sheet. Selling a fragrance, though, requires spending outside of the product to build adequate emotional value within the product.

Most design houses never take the challenge of starting their own fragrance lines in-house because of the added costs, not of the product, but building the emotional value. Companies like Estée Lauder, for example, have relationships with sales forces at major magazines allowing for discounted rates on volume of advertising pages. A one-off advertisement in a magazine could be as much or more than $30,000, depending on the magazine and its circulation. However, if Estée Lauder, or some other licensee, needed to advertise consistently for different brands, even if one brand fails, the host of other brands would offer the licensee enough diversification to offset associated losses. Moreover, Estée Lauder does not tend to make its money at the first launch of a new fragrance. In fact, most of the money to be made in the fragrance business is after a few years. Estée Lauder has significant channels for secondary distribution. After the fragrance leaves the department stores, chain stores pick them up. Estée Lauder profits mostly from its wholesaling of the original fragrance a year or two down the line rather than during the launch and first sales. In the United States, approximately 2,000 department stores exist with few new locations opening up. Adding up all of the Walgreens, CVSs, and Walmarts, you're looking at a distribution channel that may be wider than 200,000 stores and growing. As discussed previously, the dynamics of building a chain-store company vis-à-vis a department-store company have more differences than similarities with respect to budget guidelines and business models.

Frank Mori and I wanted to dissuade Donna and Steve from entering a new business without having tested the waters with licensing. Bringing a fragrance in-house when most other accouterments remained outside of our daily routine encroached on our operating capital. We had a certain amount of money allocated for future investments, but how it was invested should have remained within the bounds of the executive branch of the company. Donna and Steve, however, had their own plan.

Steve sculpted the bottle and Donna worked with others to come up with the perfume. Everyone argued against them, stating these kinds of operations should remain with those who know the field and handle the distribution on their own. I thought the bottle was innovative but impractical. Innovative because this bottle might have been the first for which you could not see the actual fragrance. The bottle was black and dark, colors in line with our advertising brands. The branding was strong. The spray mechanism, however, never functioned properly. It hadn't been properly engineered to fit the bottle. Donna went forward with launching the new product. Needless to say, the fragrance division didn't last long within the Donna Karan Company.

The next major dispute between everyone else and me had been the hiring of a president for DKNY when the company first launched. Donna, Steve, and Frank thought Michael Lichtenstein should take the position. Lichtenstein had spent some time in the fashion world as the president of a women's shoe company, far from managing a garment company. I personally liked Lichtenstein, but he was not the right candidate for the job—he had no real experience, and considering the growing size of the operations, it's difficult to hit the ground running.

Frank, though, put Donna Karan New York and Anne Klein on the same plane with Lichtenstein. Because Frank had little experience when I hired him, he thought Lichtenstein's greater experience in another leg of the business would suffice. Frank, though, disregarded the stage at which he was hired to run Anne Klein. Anne Klein was a small company when he joined. After years of working with others, Frank filled his shoes. Lichtenstein, however, did not have the same advantage of running the company from a small operation to a bigger one. He came from a small, niche operation to a much larger broader position. DKNY was growing at a tremendous pace and if he couldn't hack it, we would be the ones losing.

I argued fervently against hiring Lichtenstein, but Donna, Steve, and Frank overlooked my advice. After Lichtenstein was hired, I sat down with him and told him what I thought. I had nothing against him as a person, but I didn't think he fit the job. Maybe I shot myself in the foot for not believing in him or he didn't know what he was getting into, but in four months, Donna and Steve fired him. Later on, Lichtenstein turned against us. He opened a civil case against the company for breaking his contract. Making matters stranger, Lichtenstein asked me to testify for him because I told the other executives he was the wrong man for the job. I was summoned, and of course, I couldn't testify against my own company, so I commenced settlement negotiations with his lawyers.

Both of these anecdotes highlight one central point: Never give up too much equity to people with minimal to no management experience. Being a manager is akin to being a psychologist: You must remain vigilant of your feelings as much as your thinking. More practically, equity equates with the determination of a profit/loss structure as well as a power hierarchy. Equity changes business relationships much like money can muddy a family's dynamic. More equity means more power in the corporate world, and sometimes more power does not result in greater margins or success. Alternatively, an equity split among numerous partners can obscure the vision initiating a project. When Donna and Steve started the fragrance line, they did something out of character for the Donna Karan Company as well as out of character with management. However, when management only owns half and not a share more, little can be done at an impasse. I believe in listening to everyone's opinions to help form my own, but straying too far from an original venture is neither a productive nor lucrative task. This one lesson was perhaps the most expensive one of my entire career.

Pay Me Now and Pay Me Later

An important life lesson is in this chapter. No one enjoys going to lawyers. Some may even prefer a root canal to a meeting with an attorney. In fact, some intended marriages break up because of the pain involved in a prenuptial agreement. However, lawyers are necessary even when people like and trust one another. Even family will fight over an unclear will if one sibling seems to be the recipient of special favors.

(continued)

(continued)

One wise sage explained the lesson: "Pay me now or pay me later." Tomio could have avoided much grief and money if he had had a legal agreement when they launched the partnership. So, pay the lawyers now and you avoid losing money and having pain. It is cheaper than the fallout from an agreement. Tomio believed Donna would stay in the design area. He didn't consider the emergence of her husband. A well-structured legal agreement would have avoided this dispute and provided the boundaries of each partner. For every strength, a weakness exists. Tomio with his insight and courage was able to build an empire in apparel. However, he couldn't predict the future and how people change with challenging circumstances.

Finally, I would like to note the possibility for a cultural bias in this sidebar. The Japanese hold different relationships with lawyers than do many Western Europeans and Americans. In Japan, they are only used when necessary. In the United States, lawyers remain on call like an emergency room surgeon. In fact, there may be more lawyers in Washington, DC, than in the entire nation of Japan.

Mortimer R. Feinberg, PhD

CHAPTER 18

The Initial Public Offering of Donna Karan International

Opening a discourse on what I would have done differently is an interesting launching pad. More cases than not, managers tend to laud themselves and allow pride to overtake memory. However, a number of interesting lessons emerged in my time as a manager of two large fashion companies in the United States that have applications beyond such geopolitical boundaries. Of course, different cultures react and respond differently, and this may be why multinational corporations like Toyota prefer to hire local managers in the United States to handle operations rather than import them from Japan. Having a leg up on cultural nuances ranging from working conditions to employee expectations is a big advantage.

The scope of the book has been historical. However, as my narrative comes to a close, I would like to reflect a bit on what has been discussed while providing further insight. To do so, I would like to delve a little deeper into Donna Karan New York and the departure of Takihyo Inc. (Takihyo) from that entity. Over the course of 10 years, Donna Karan blossomed into the household name that it is today. Although there have been more positive than negative points, the negative ones in the story demand attention to supplement future endeavors for readers and as a means by which I can learn. In other words, I would like to return to the Donna Karan story to learn from my mistakes and develop solutions to combat them rather than terminating the discussion on a purely historical note leaving readers to speculate.

The Donna Karan Company underwent three primary stages. The first stage was the startup. Other than the aforementioned work with Peter Arnell, the branding genius, there was a lot of legwork on both sides of the partnership. When I fired Donna to start the new company, she had to learn some of the necessary elements to running the company. Donna didn't have any previous management experience; she only knew how to run the design team. Though this skill is important when it comes deciding what garments to make and how to thread seasons together to create a uniform and appealing look for consumers, the managerial decision making was a bit lacking. There was some overlap. Donna could make design decisions that I couldn't, but I would suggest certain color palates or styles to Donna so she could create a new line that was cohesive with the brand.

There were disputes among top management that at times could not be settled by one person. Instead, multiple opinions appeared on various issues, and no one had the upper hand. I try not to regret any of the decisions I have made before, but I prefer to learn from my mistakes. Donna Karan New York was a 50/50 partnership. With any new venture, I have tried to stray away from an equity split down the middle especially when I have such a vested interest.

Before organizing the company, Donna and I were discussing how the company should be managed. Takihyo, being Frank and myself, would have total control over all financial and managerial elements of the business, and Donna would have total control of the design room. This was our verbal contract, but we never put it into writing. When Steve came into the mix, the dynamic changed dramatically. The operating agreement should have spelled out the split in managerial and financial decisions. Instead, Donna could have Steve make decisions for her and would use her equity position to leverage the execution of whatever plan Takihyo did not condone. As a result, even if Takihyo held half of the company, we could not control the direction of the business without engaging legal counsel, and at that point, such a new company could unravel over lowered morale resulting from indecisiveness among management. There is nothing worse than having hundreds of people relying on you and you can't give them a straight answer. By the second phase of Donna Karan New York, we were building up a new brand of diffusion line: DKNY.

If I were to do it all over again, I would have reconsidered the terms of the operating agreement. If the partnership were an investor and a manager, a split down the middle was no problem. Provided that the investor did not meddle with the manager, there would be no cause for concern. However, this 50/50 partnership dichotomized members from varied experience levels and areas of expertise. From the beginning of any new startup in which I am manager and financier, I ensure the equity position is levered in my favor even if marginally. A 2 percent difference could have made a world of difference at Donna Karan New York. If a point over partnership distribution is debated, this could be easily mitigated by issuing phantom shares to the minority partner. The equity split 51/49 would only be in place for tougher decisions.

I mention this because Donna Karan was growing at a tremendous pace. Whenever a company prospers, wealth begets greed and selfishness. It may be a part of human nature. If I can make a dress and sell it for double the price to consumers, capitalism applauds regardless of state and creed. The majority of my narrative on the Donna Karan Company focused on the downsides of the business. I was so concerned with losing money that I forgot about what would happen if I made money. Everyone and everything was against me on the managerial end, so I did my best to make the company a success. In so doing, I misplaced some of my energies. Everyone was against starting a new company with Donna because Anne Klein had been going so well. So I spent most of my time defending my arguments and making arrangements to protect the new venture from all of the problems that could arise.

Once the DKNY line was launched, consumers only wanted more. We could only raise prices so much without squelching the demand, so we needed to capitalize future growth. However, our current assets shrank considerably on a cyclical basis. Every new season was difficult for us because we had to come up with the cash to pay for the next one, which was significantly bigger than the last. After taxes, the company's income could only afford so much further growth. At this point, Donna Karan New York had its first major upside problem, which I had previously neglected.

I could do little on this front and had few options. I could bring in another partner, but the amount of equity needing to be sold would not be in the favor of Donna or Takihyo. We would end up having to sell a business that we started, and we would be left with only a small portion of earnings from a company growing at an exponential rate. Though venture capitalists may think of this as a successful exit strategy, I saw more potential in the company and it was so new that I couldn't abandon it so soon. I didn't want to lose money because we were making so much.

First, while we were successful initially, we feared not being able to keep up with demand. Since we were designing and manufacturing seasons ahead, we needed capital for various material commitments ranging from a host of new fabrics and accouterments to inspire the design team to money to pay our invoices and working capital requirements. Our problem before starting Anne Klein II had been capital restraints. Our growth had been so fast that our capital demands outpaced our earnings. To fuel this momentum, we only had a few options. Our growth was tremendous and we were running out of money to fuel the forward momentum. This was a good problem that we could not have foreseen.

At DKNY, we ran into the same problem a little down the road. Neither Donna nor I wanted to add new partners with money. We did not want to issue new debt because the company was graded BBB. If we were to issue debt, we would be required to pay about 10 to 12 percent on the bond. This would not have hurt the company, but it seemed to be a steep price to pay for operating capital. So Donna and Takihyo were left with one other option: go public.

Entering the public market is a great financial tactic if done properly. Outside money pours into the company to furnish funding for future endeavors. Because there are many different investors instead of one or two other partners, power within the company is diluted. Donna and Takihyo would still hold a significant control of the company. Additionally, with a public company comes more attention and brand recognition. We would be able to raise further funds in the future through equity issuance as well as provide shareholders with dividends or share buybacks once the company reached a kind of stasis in the marketplace of developed nations. From this perspective, we had a lot to gain and little to lose.

However, the initial public offering (IPO) was a harried endeavor. We started working with Bear Stearns and Merrill Lynch for the launch in 1997. They were pushing us to go public because they were concerned about their bottom lines as publicly traded companies. For the investment banks, mergers and acquisitions (M&As) as well as IPOs offer a significant amount of their bread and butter. It is in their best interest to get companies to go public. Once done, they take their fees and move on. So, every day, people from Merrill Lynch and Bear Stearns were at the office pushing everyone to get everything from a prospectus drafted to coming up with numbers for a starting bid price for the stock. Once the stock launched, and we were public, we took a step back and let the market decide what would happen next.

Going public could continue our business. In this sense, the IPO was a success. The stock was launched and shot up about 10 percent in the first weeks. However, shortly after, the equity tanked. There were a number of reasons for this, some of which arose out of not having enough time to prepare our prospectus as well as to iron out details between Donna, Steve, and Takihyo. Steve and Donna used this to their advantage and we did not have time to argue with them before the IPO. The investment banks, with Bear Stearns as the lead underwriter, wanted to hurry the offering.

Taking note of the shareholders' interest is important, and regardless of how little their votes may count, they tend to add up, especially when market consensus shifts from bullish to bearish. My narrative places the Anne Klein story before the Donna Karan New York story for good reason. One started much before the other; however, some overlap occurred but for the sake of simplicity were illustrated one after the other. Before we sold Anne Klein to Arthur Levine at Kaspar was about the same time that we were considering going public.

The Anne Klein Company was in trouble because Donna was gone, but the brand and operating company still had room to grow and a relatively healthy balance sheet for such an old-fashioned house. So, we had kept Anne Klein on the wayside as an entity, which Frank and I owned. However, once talks of bringing Donna Karan public were initiated, Frank and I had to exit most executive meetings because of what the SEC would consider a conflict of interests. Although

Anne Klein and Donna Karan were two entirely separate identities in the public eye and in the design room, the SEC still considered them competition. Indeed, some overlap occurred, but most of it was negligible. Nonetheless, because one company was privately owned and the other was about to go public, a host of new restrictions were put in place against Takihyo's best interest. From a legal view, Anne Klein was a competitor to Donna Karan New York so any information regarding Donna Karan New York could not be leaked into the Anne Klein Company. Since we held significant interests in both companies, all Frank and I could do was sit around and hope for the best. These regulations against our involvement in the company significantly hurt our chances of a successful public launch.

In short, Frank and I could do little to change Donna and Steve's minds regarding the guidelines listed in the initial prospectus. The blinding speed at which the investment banks were pushing us to go public didn't help either because neither Steve nor Donna saw any imminent problems with what they were suggesting. As I mentioned, the banks didn't care about the company going public; they cared about their fees. The fees only came once the company went public, and after that, there was no more support despite the contracts because we paid the invoices. In a way, Donna Karan International's failure as public equity best illustrated that when it comes to money and people outside of the business, managers need to be careful, especially because all people are only interested when it comes to their own financial well-being rather than that of others.

The saddest part of this whole debacle was that Donna Karan International, as we renamed the company, was still making money. The balance sheets and cash flow statements were strong, perhaps a lot stronger than many other companies that were publicly traded at the time. The value of the brand wasn't going anywhere as long as the managers didn't make major changes to the business model and the design teams continued to innovate and grow. Even though shareholders lost a lot of money in those few months, at the end of the day, ownership in the company was still worth a lot more than where the stock ended up. Though efficient market theory is still discussed today, from a manager's perspective, it remains only a theory with little basis in reality.

Making matters more complicated was the differentiation between the brand and the company. In most cases, when a company is acquired, the name is bought separately from the operating company, or only one or the other is purchased. Frank and I gave Donna the right to keep her name: This made sense to me because I would never imagine that Donna would sell it. However, for legal purposes, the name Donna Karan was kept in a separate entity to avoid other complications. Donna put the name in an entity she named after her daughter. So, Takihyo did not own the name, and we held the operating company although we were responsible for the company's branding, marketing, and publicity from scratch. This point is important because the final sale of Donna Karan International included the sale of Donna's name, but Takihyo did not and could not benefit from it.

To me, Donna did the unthinkable. Along with the company we started from scratch, she sold her name after the company went public, tanked, and was resold. The investment banks suggested Donna take the royalties from the operating company and deposit them into Gabrielle Studio, the company that owned the Donna Karan New York brand name. We had created Gabrielle Studio because if anything happened to the operating company (bankruptcy, litigation, etc.), the Donna Karan name would remain unaffected. Since Gabrielle Studio owned the brand name, the company existed separately from the operating company. However, because of the initial structure, the input from lawyers, CPAs, and company executives bringing all the risks to the fore, the brand name would need to be saved even in the worst-case scenarios. Takihyo could not own the name because it would be considered an asset to Takihyo and could be lost in litigation. However, if Donna owned a company in which the name had been housed, the brand name could not be taken away because the name was her own. I never thought Donna and Steve would be the only ones to benefit from the brand name, as the purpose was to shield us all.

Louis Vuitton purchased Donna Karan International after the stock entered bankruptcy territory trading for a tenth of the IPO price. The massive French luxury conglomerate paid nearly twice as much for the brand as they did for the company. Louis Vuitton got the operating company for a real bargain considering the cash flows, partly due to John Idol's role as the company's president before the sale as a fantastic accounting and managerial mind, future growth prospects, and good timing. Looking back, perhaps I should have kept the name within the company.

When all was said and done, I was still in the black on the balance sheet, but I wound up losing a lot of money when the company was grossly devalued in the markets in addition to losing on the sale of the brand that Takihyo had created with Peter Arnell. Other than altering the equity split, I should have spent more time concentrating on both scenarios: if we became tremendously profitable and if we failed. I only focused on the failure of this company because of the negativity surrounding me. This led me to make cautious decisions, but they lacked the broad strokes necessary to take the reins with such a successful company. Even though the Donna Karan New York brand is still alive and well today, great entrepreneurial success does not always equate with a perfect execution.

On Business Maturity

In the previous chapter, I discussed the common occurrence of subordinates and peers having the attitude of "pay me now, pay me later." By no means does this approach to handling colleagues engender a desire for repeat business. After the sale of Donna Karan International, Tomio Taki no longer had any business relations with Donna Karan or Steve Weiss. Donna remained a chief designer at the company and Taki went on to other ventures such as attending to his equitable interest in the Honolulu Country Club in Hawaii and his various board positions. However, it is inevitable that everyone will suffer from a colleague's selfish behavior at some point or another, but the seasoned manager will have a sense of business maturity and be capable of recognizing it in others. What is "business maturity"?

A smart manager doesn't always recognize maturity. Intelligence and maturity are not necessarily related. A person could recite the Encyclopedia Britannica by heart—and still be infantile in his or her emotions. All of us have known brilliant people who are like children in controlling their feelings, in their overpowering need for affection from everybody they meet, in the way they handle themselves and others, or in their response to frustration. However, brilliance of intellect is no handicap to mature development. Evidence suggests quite the contrary: bright people tend to effect superior emotional and social adjustments.

No executive is capable of reacting to all situations and all aspects of his life with complete maturity 100 percent of the time. However, executives do handle many of their problems maturely. The qualities usually found in the mature, then, can be pinpointed. No single individual is likely to have all of them— but all are worth striving for. I have been able to identify a handful of signs to recognizing emotional maturity.

The most effective executives are those who have a fairly good view of their strengths and weaknesses. This aspect may be the only necessary element for an executive's success. Only the mature executive will surround him- or herself with people to complement those weaknesses because recognizing deficiencies leads to addressing and overcoming them. Consequently, the mature executive has a respect for difference and recognizes that each individual has his/her own set of strengths and deficiencies. Molding employees to your own image is never the task of a mature, seasoned manager as this behavior only leads to contempt and tension in the workplace.

Most importantly, however, may be the manager's endurance. We have all known intelligent and capable executives who have failed because they didn't have enough emotional and physical stamina. Ecclesiastes noted that the race is not necessarily to the swift. The challenge is to keep running. So, too, in business, what often counts is the ability to work consistently long and hard, especially under pressure and after disappointing setbacks.

Fatigue leads to a loss of efficiency, impaired initiative, distorted judgment, skewed perception of time, and heightened anxiety. Fatigue also erodes subjective standards of performance. As we grow more tired, we are ready to settle for less quality and accuracy. The mature manager will instruct subordinates and colleagues to note which activities relax and recharge them. Keeping a sense of humor, in particular an ability to laugh at yourself, goes hand-in-hand. An able business leader knows

(continued)

(continued)

how to help his group discharge their tension by injecting an appropriate note of levity. Not much is understood about how humor works, but it seems to relieve stress and release constructive energies.

As with most problems bedeviling executives, much remains to be learned. We can expect a continuing demand for placebos and fast-cure, over-the-counter remedies. However, the ultimate source of a manager's ability to stay the course must be self-discipline. Only then can he or she share the boast of a genius like Louis Pasteur: "My greatest strength lies solely in my tenacity."

Mortimer R. Feinberg, PhD

Wrap Up America

Respice, Adspice, Prospice

Going through 75 years of my life in just over 200 pages is not as simple as it may appear. Many of my stories, for lack of direct relevance, had to be excised from this latest draft, but I believe the purpose of this book has been fulfilled. Reciting every event would have its value in a fragmented way, but the most important lessons of my life are contained here. My experiences in other countries, like Israel, South Korea, France, and Italy speak to the varied cultures and communities with which I have had the pleasure and privilege to work. I have been able to draw new lines of contrast and comparison among the different nations, some of which are obvious and others more nuanced.

For example, I learned that the South Korean business mentality is more similar to the American one than to Western Europe or anywhere else in the Far East. There is an aggression among executives that one may only find in these two countries. When South Korean businesspeople want something, they do everything in their power to get it. In the United States, we see a similarity but it is couched in a different set of cultural values and ethics. Israel and Japan share similar business cultures as well. The kibbutz mentality of keeping business in the family extends to almost all areas of Israeli industry. The value of currency takes a lower priority to the quality of life for the individual. In Japan, business is the employee and the employee is the business. Managers traditionally don't take drastic measures to get the job done. In Israel, I have found it to be similar.

A number of years ago, I befriended Meir Amit. As a young man, Amit became the head of the Mossad and the Aman (military intelligence). As his career advanced, he became the head of Koor Industries, which at first was an arm of the Histadrut (government labor union of Israel) and later become the massive conglomerate that it is today. Amit proposed I take a trip to see how a kibbutz functions and see if I could help some of these economically failing socialist communities. After multiple trips, I learned that the cost of manpower to create a product that the kibbutz would sell was far greater than the income derived from the sale. Additionally, the cost of living for each individual member of the kibbutz was far greater than revenues produced. The members of the kibbutz had a limited understanding of the workings of capitalism—and why would they? Members of the kibbutz have ancestral lineages that go generations back. These people have no real experience with capital and, therefore, no sense of economic value. Today, kibbutzim are primarily supported by the Israeli government as cultural institutions, I believe, because changing the way they operate was not an option as it would alter the culture.

In Japan, we see similarities. Traditional Japanese companies don't fire employees even if they underperform. In a way, the Japanese company is like a kibbutz: once a member, always a member. Japanese companies are hesitant to change. Indeed, it is safe to say that the Japanese nation as a whole is hesitant to change. The failure of many Japanese companies in their real estate ventures of the 1980s until the bubble-burst derives from a business culture with no conception of the outside world of capital. Japanese businesses didn't understand the importance of altering how one does business abroad even if it was to their benefit. Israeli companies, like the kibbutz, traditionally do not like outsourcing.

I once consulted for an Israeli refrigerator company that was a division of Koor Industries. At the time, a handful of different models were in production. Many were not selling. I told them to focus on the ones that were and discard the others. The executives understood the need to focus their energies, but did not want to lose business. I proposed they buy refrigerators from an Italian manufacturer wholesale and resell them. They hesitated to take my suggestion, but after review, they realized they needed to do this, otherwise their operations would fail. The cost of manufacturing too many refrigerators in-house was far greater than the reward, and if another manufacturer was making a similar model, it made more economic sense to resell that model despite cultural inclinations. Getting these executives past this first stumbling block was one of my first successes in Israel. For Japan and Israel, looking for help from the outside for whatever reason is an obstacle.

These comparisons could be an entire book on their own—perhaps my next project. Sketching a quick meta-examination of culture's impact on industry holds importance to this narrative because I want to use these short anecdotes as the backbone for the analysis of the past, present, and future of the United States. Having seen firsthand how the rest of the world (dys)functions has opened my eyes to what needs to change and what needs to remain the same. Since the past 40 years of my life have been in the United States, I feel a responsibility to outline my thoughts: respice, adspice, prospice.

Although I had direct contact with Americans almost all of my life, I did not move to the United States until around 1980. I began doing business in the United States in the 1970s and slowly moved to where I saw the most opportunity. Japan had begun to falter a bit and Takihyo Ltd. was suffering from the broader economic conditions. I saw more value in owning an American fashion company and I had a handful of ideas to implement, delineated in the second part of this book. I have discussed much of my thoughts on the past as a result, but I have drawn no ink on the present problems and what I believe to be their future resolution.

Unless you were in a cave for the past three years, you would have witnessed the worst economic meltdown since the Great Depression. Unemployment shot through the roof and has hovered at around 10 percent for the past year, double the historical average of 5 percent. The largest market in the United States, housing, imploded. Banks were lending money they didn't anticipate getting back. There was an assumption that real estate prices would continue to rise. (Does this sound similar to the Japanese bubble that burst in the 1980s?) In many cases with limited to no documentation, banks would lend money at adjustable rates to people who could never pay it back. The first couple of years would be easy sailing for the debtor. The loan would then reset, and by that point, the banks assumed the property value would have risen to a point that refinancing the loan would be the next step. Kicking this can down the road lasted for some time until refinancing was no longer an option for the debtors. Predatory lending occurred in many cases in which property owners took a mortgage after having owned the property outright so the bank could seemingly raise its bottom line. When real estate prices stopped rising, the loans reset, and the market turned inside-out. Debtors could no longer refinance, and they could not pay the new rates. Real estate went to hell in a handbasket. Since the real estate market is the largest market in the United States, everything else followed.

The government's response to this crisis was and remains a bit weak. The Obama administration and Ben Bernanke's Federal Reserve have pumped tons of money into a system without real significant legislative reform. The government has chosen to print more money and buy more of its own debt in the hopes that it will keep inflation under 2 percent and spur investor confidence in the equity markets. Hopefully, this will work, but it looks like another kicking of the can down the road rather than replacing the rotten foundations. The debt-to-capital ratios for the banks have improved, but few loans are being given so there is minimal leverage in the markets. People aren't buying houses and many people are out of work. Consumer spending has been significantly cut back even by those with the money to spend. Like Japan, the United States is not consuming the way it had before. Consumers have become more price-conscious as well. With the likes of Amazon, Newegg, Google, and eBay, along with a host of other niche online marketplaces, physical retail stores have taken a hit with the exception of dollar stores and bulk grocery stores like Costco and Walmart. Another unfortunate similarity between the United States and Japan is the fear of a future deflationary environment.

Making matters worse, the United States also has no real industry to speak of. Americans hardly manufacture anything here and most US businesses outsource to other countries. Like Japan, the United States has an aging population. The figures don't read as dramatically as the Japanese problem, but if nothing is done to combat this, the United States will age and all the fears I have for Japan will become an American reality. How can one go about fixing such deep-seated issues?

Considering how events have played out, it appears that the best route is to take the bumpy road of inflation. The Fed should monitor inflation so it doesn't get out of control, but inflation will allow wages to rise. Inflation may be the key to increasing the size of the American workforce because the less the dollar is worth, the more dollars one may receive and more money will be available for labor. Although there would be a rise of general wages, this does not mean there is a need to increase minimum wage. If the dollar is worth less tomorrow and minimum wage stays the same, many companies may begin to find it profitable to begin manufacturing in the United States again. Other than the automobile industry, the United States could begin to sustain its own domestic markets for goods. This hope equates with a strong, stable, and self-sustaining United States.

Another major problem with the US economic system is trade protectionism. Though many believe trade protectionism has helped America become the economic powerhouse it is today, I believe they are wrong. The United States is too careful about what comes into the country and indifferent as to what leaves it. For example, Japanese beef may be the best beef in the world. American beef is rated second for many other countries, and it lags in comparison to Japanese beef. The US government has made strict quotas for beef to prop up the industry. Without this crutch, the government fears the beef industry would shrivel up. I believe that at first, the US beef industry could take a hit. However, increased competition in the beef market might increase the quality of the beef in the United States to a level that could compare to Japanese beef. History has shown that no matter how hard times become, innovation yields better and more economic solutions. Beef and every other industry suffering from the misguidance of trade protectionism would benefit from increased competition.

The execution of trade protectionism is closely related to labor unions in the United States. Even though labor unions provide a service to American workers, it is a double-edged sword. The labor union has developed a "not-my-job" mentality in the United States in terms of shielding responsibilities. US workers are given responsibilities but because one union represents this job and another the next, workers don't overlap their responsibilities with others for fear of stepping on one another's toes. This viewpoint, I believe, destroys the relationship the workers have with their colleagues as well as their company. There is no sense of team within the company; instead, the team is the union and allegiance to that union is paramount to the company. So, if the company fails as a result of a union member not wanting to help another union worker, no accountability occurs on the part of the worker. The brunt of it falls on the shareholders or owners of the company. Since legislation differs from state to state, this level of responsibility changes with location. If teamwork could be emphasized as a part of labor union education, collaboration with companies could be more streamlined. Another problem with unions is the price one is required to pay. Part of the reason the American auto companies needed to be bailed out was the requirements unions had on these companies for their workers.

Toyota and other foreign automobile manufacturers have cut their labor expenses nearly in half by setting up plants outside of Michigan. Instead of paying union workers somewhere around $80 per hour, Toyota and others have reduced that expense to around $40 per hour. In both cases, these workers make quite a bit of money, but the auto unions in Michigan had a major hand in the unraveling of the business. The best solution for business owners may be to disband unions altogether so workers can compete with one another in the marketplace for jobs rather than be handed one despite past performance. Of course, unions would benefit workers if they were more friendly to business and less self-serving. For instance, how labor unions strike tends to hurt businesses, particularly if businesses cannot afford to pay new wage raises or other benefits. In many ways, the failures of the kibbutz system parallel those of companies forced into constraining union relationships. If and when unions understand how they can benefit the worker as well as the companies to which they are tied, a more economically viable solution could be found. Though I would be in favor of disbanding unions altogether and increasing competition among workers for jobs, which may increase productivity and/or the quality of work, I don't see this as a reality.

I have many other qualms with how the US economy and industry functions, but the last one I'd like to discuss is taxation. Everyone knows that federal, state, and city governments are running out of money. Credit default swaps, which are insurance against the default of a bond, for the state of California are more expensive than those of some third-world countries. Social Security is a joke and the new health bill will probably hurt the medical industry more than help it 50 years from now if nothing is done. As I discussed at the end of Part 1 of this book, my prescription for Japanese taxation holds true for the United States as well. I believe the United States could gain from dissolution of the current system and a small city/state/federal deduction from all banking transactions. The only exception to this rule would be to leave real estate taxes the same. This solution may wind up killing a ton of jobs at the Internal Revenue Service and accounting/auditing firms, but at the end of the day, this kind of a system will be more beneficial for companies, individuals, and the state.

Conclusion

Zennovation in Retrospect

When I began writing my father's book, I had some knowledge of the financial operations of a handful of public companies. I had been reading many books, research reports, shareholder and partner letters, and Securities and Exchange Commission (SEC) filings to expand my knowledge base on how to invest and in what to invest. That research has proved quite meaningful to managing my own portfolio of public equities as well as offering some insight into my emotional reactions to financial gains and losses. However, none of that work prepared me to be an entrepreneur the way the experience of writing this book has. My father has been a tutor of sorts in helping me learn about day-to-day business operations.

I treated writing the book much like an academic pursuit. Researching my father's life through one-on-one interviews offered me his approach to entrepreneurship, but I was also lucky enough to talk with other academics, business leaders, and psychologists. In tandem, these conversations opened my eyes to the art of entrepreneurship—I found the challenges and the thought processes behind company creation, branding, and marketing absolutely fascinating.

As early as high school, I enjoyed drawing, painting, and screen printing. My interests later expanded to include photography and video art. As a young student, I was fortunate enough to be in a handful of exhibitions, ranging from a small mom-and-pop ice cream store to an exhibition for young emerging talent at the Norman Rockwell Museum. My artistic activities, however, I treated as nothing more than a hobby. I attended Vassar College and studied philosophy, religion, political science, and Italian literature. I never stepped into a studio art class nor did I think to pursue art or art history.

I moved back home to New York and found an apartment. I matriculated into New York University, where I earned a master's degree from the Graduate School of Arts and Science. This period was one of intensive study, but occasionally I found myself going to more art openings and exhibitions. I became friendly with an art dealer who represented only New York–based emerging artists. He was going to store some artwork but asked if I'd like to borrow something for my apartment since I had just moved into a new place. I agreed and for about a year, I had a fantastic work by the mid-career artist Johnathan Cramer hanging in my living room. After, I had to return the piece and had a blank wall to fill, so I decided to make a mixed media piece integrating my love for painting with photography.

The dealer came to my house to see the new work. He fell in love with it and asked if I could make more. From that point on, he began representing my work. However, his operation was very small and it was clear he needed help. I had been inadvertently developing a diverse set of skills, ranging from my interest in computer science to design and photography. After a few exhibitions, I partnered with my dealer. We worked together for some time but then had a bit of a falling out; however, I had learned a lot about the business, everything from exhibition production and lighting to art handling. I didn't want to give up the business quite yet but I needed to move on from that partnership.

It was the middle of 2008. The recession had begun to take hold, causing various economic challenges regarding any- and everything involved in starting a gallery. I decided to jump in head first, figuring that given the financial climate I'd be at an advantage as one of the few people negotiating new contracts with advertisers, architects, contractors, print shops, public relations specialists, and so on. This was the first time I had made a major commitment of capital, and it may have been the worst economic downturn I will witness. While this instinct grew out of my enjoyment in public equity investment, various readings on finance, and an understanding gleaned from attending financial conferences, the structure and basis for what would become my new gallery stemmed from the entrepreneurial spirit my father and his colleagues instilled in me while writing this book. This chapter is not about my father, but it *is* about the application of his ideas—what he learned from some of his failures, and everything in between that he has taught me about how to found a start-up. The gallery is still new and fresh with its own growing pains, but in this chapter, I hope to illustrate that the concepts put forth in this book have applications beyond the fashion and textile industries.

Although my business is very different from Takihyo's, there are certain fundamental principles that translate across the industries. In Chapter 18, my father discusses the problems inherent not only in 50/50 equity splits but also in the downsides of creating a lucrative venture. My father learned the hard way that verbal contracts hold no legitimacy in the American legal system. However, beginning a venture where employees feel part of the organization from top to bottom introduces new challenges. In my father's case, at first Donna Karan was to have control only over the design room, but later on in the partnership her husband was given an executive role. There are three different risks here.

The first risk had been that all financial support came from the management team, but management could lose control in a standstill among partners. Donna was given 50 percent sweat equity on paper and in a verbal agreement the right to control only the design room. The written agreement left Donna with not only the equity power to make decisions but also the capacity to overrule the other partners. In many cases, a creative type should not also have the duties of a managerial or fiduciary executive because this combination of skill sets is akin to mixing oil and water—nothing gets done and there are poor decisions on both sides of the equation. In the world of fashion, there are very few people who are capable of both managing and designing.

And the second risk came from this loss of power among management. There was the insertion of an executive, undermining managerial control. Because of Donna's equity position, she had the right to place whomever she chose as a company officer—she did so with her husband, who had little experience in the field. Donna's voice in the boardroom then doubled. Although at first she was to have control only of the design room, she now had greater influence. As noted in previous chapters, this change of events posed new problems not only to my father but also to the communication among executives and the design team, which led to the failed initial public offering and subsequent sale to Louis Vuitton Moet Hennessey (LVMH).

Lastly, Donna's name was the company. There was nothing wrong with naming the Donna Karan Company after its primary designer, but neither my father nor Frank foresaw that Donna would sell the rights to her own name. This only emerged later as a problem with the initial public offering. When LVMH showed interest in purchasing the company, the group had to buy not only the operating company but also a holding company whose primary asset was the rights to use "Donna Karan." Sequestering her name in a separate company, as my father had recommended, tripled Donna's take upon the LVMH acquisition, but also denied the liquidation event to the financiers and executive management.

These three points, I have discussed *ad absurdum* with my father. He talks about his faults in managing the Donna Karan Company as those in which he prepared only for downside risk rather than upside risk. Because Donna Karan did so well, my father never thought his upside take would have been decimated and divided by his partners. In my newest venture, I have (hopefully) rightfully applied the outcome of these discussions to address these three points in the following ways so as to protect myself on both the downside and the upside.

More particularly, when starting my gallery, I was interested in finding someone with whom I could work well. I needed a complement to my style and a supplement to my ken. I needed someone who not only had experience within the art world, but I also searched for legacy, good taste, and a willingness to grow with the company rather than on the side of the company. Experience speaks for itself, but legacy provides downside risk that many other ventures do not. I wanted an employee who was young enough to want to grow and to work with me to create an image, a brand, and, more important, a community—a lifestyle. Legacy followed by a piqued interest in the field can determine one's sustainability within the field. Whomever I would hire would have a strong understanding of how the art world works—unable to be disenchanted and so engaged that no other line of work would satisfy him or her.

I also needed additional access to the art world. The leverage that an employee with all of these traits could offer would enhance the recognition and reputation of the new gallery and supply press exposure and an existing client base to boot. How could I do all of this while not breaking the bank and how could I find someone to meet exactly my expectations and hopes? Word-of-mouth seemed to be the only way to find the right person, but when I found her I knew the deal would need to be sweet enough to keep her interest.

Luckily, I found Rebecca Heidenberg. After asking countless people if they knew anyone who would meet my criteria, I finally asked the right person. I suppose this is all it takes. Before we began working together, I interviewed many people for the position of director of the new gallery. Some were either hot or cold; some seemed too self-serving and self-interested to want to become part of a larger process. Some were in the art world as the children of known, established artists, and others were hungry for a job. We were, in fact, at the nadir of the recession (provided the Euro-crisis does not implode and plunge the US economy into another, perhaps deeper, recessionary period). For the art world, everything seemed to be falling apart, but some still seemed picky and others were desperate.

Returning to Rebecca, she met the initial criteria. She had been in the business about 10 years, and her mother has been an art dealer for decades. Rebecca worked for a number of galleries, but her skills as a curator and her ability to source difficult-to-find works come from a life spent in the art world meeting collectors, curators, dealers, developers, and others. Growing up with a successful art dealer as a parent has empowered her not to replicate but to create her own path with the strength of a life's worth of contacts and a strong reputation behind her. Finding and convincing her to work for me capped the first of the three risks outlined earlier.

I capped the first risk by not partnering with her at all; however, our agreement states I am to relinquish a 10 percent stake to her when the company becomes cash-flow positive and net debts have been paid. The 10 percent places Rebecca in a minority shareholder position, which is not quite the same as the 15 percent or higher stake a court would rule in favor of if we were to become wildly successful. I not only finance all operations in the gallery but also provide support on every level of operations—giving away 10 percent is generous, but enough to comfort Rebecca.

Keeping Rebecca at a 10 percent equity position then limits her right to place other associates. I also have a strict policy to not hire those with whom any of us has a personal or familial relationship. There is some gray area among certain artists with which the gallery lightly flirts, but artists are not management nor are they a part of the curatorial branding. Moreover, we would never curate a show with an artist we do not believe shows talent and works well within the framework of how the gallery is branded and marketed. As a result, there is a limited loss of control. However, this does not mean I have painted Rebecca in a corner and given her no room to grow. Rebecca's career is meant to mature alongside the gallery's growth. I want someone to grow with me in this gallery project.

I have named the gallery "RH Gallery"—using Rebecca's initials and thereby underlining her role as the face of the gallery. Naming the gallery after her also further leverages her potential for growth alongside my endeavors in the art world. Having her name on the gallery gives Rebecca greater incentive to make the project work. Although some may criticize me for not risking opening a gallery using my own name, I have found a means by which to leverage her contacts, her relationship with her mother, and her trust. The latter, perhaps, being the most complicated. The act of letting someone handle the curatorial element of the business as well as letting her receive the lion's share of the credit places the "high" of our potential successes in her hands but still leaves me holding the risk of loss.

Provided this idea is mutually understood, we act to hedge one another not only as potential business partners but also as complementary skill sets in the gallery environment and art industry as a whole. In a way, offering Rebecca a chance without the need to put up her own capital to do what she loves limits my risk as well as her own. The only other potential problem that could arise is if Rebecca chooses to do business outside of the gallery—taking revenues away from the gallery to put money in pocket. Although this risk is legitimate and difficult to police, it is also outlined in our agreement that she is not to make any sales of art outside of our gallery. In short, she can do what she has been destined to do, and I can help her reach that place. The second and third risks, discussed previously, are addressed in her treatment as an associate of the company.

Because I am the only one injecting capital, if I chose to stop, so too would all operations. There might be some outstanding bills that I would have to address, but the exposure to loss would be limited to what has been spent within the gallery as well as the cost of returning inventory and finding a tenant for the space. Although the Donna Karan Company was a far more complex operation on a day-to-day basis and much larger in structure, there are many comparisons to be made with operating a gallery; because I oversee every dollar earned and spent at the gallery, there is no room for the mismanagement of funds or the addition of unwanted voices. Also, I do not allow others to dictate the hiring process. I am very interested in hearing what others have to say about prospective employees, but I am more willing to take responsibility for a hire that fails if I was the one who made the final decision to hire the person. As noted in Chapter 17 with the lawsuit regarding Michael Lichtenstein's firing, major hiring decisions should be left to management rather than associates. Associates tend to have less skin in the game and even if they don't always get along with one another, if a better product or service results, everyone will learn to get along or get replaced.

Within the first months of opening the gallery, I had somewhat high employee turnover. This was due to two primary factors. First, although I was paying competitively with the art industry, I was not paying competitively as a whole. In many cases, this doesn't seem to matter as high salary is not an expectation of the employee for a cultural establishment—at least not a new gallery. Second, some hires were somewhat rushed and I never got a chance to vet them out with the other associates. Combined, these two elements led to a couple of poor judgments. Now, before anyone is hired, everyone meets with the prospective employee to make sure there is good chemistry among the group. If cooperation doesn't exist, at least at a professional level, nothing gets done.

The third major risk I have addressed in my new venture, as mentioned earlier, is related to what I learned from the loss my father suffered by allowing Donna Karan to place ownership of her name in a separate entity. I hold all the rights to RH Gallery within a separate entity so in case of a sale or dissolution, I can reuse the brand if need be in the future. In most possible scenarios, a rebirth of the brand would never occur in the same industry without Rebecca, but in the case that we would have to close the space, a restructuring could take place.

This way of structuring the gallery's business, for "upside" protection, was just one of many practical ways I was able to apply the knowledge I'd gathered over a lifetime of observing my father's business dealings. During the process of writing this book, a couple other items of note came to mind. One was that when starting a new business, equity is free provided you place your own name or the name of your company in the articles of organization. There are no further capital requirements to suggest equity is to be transferred elsewhere. In a low-interest-rate environment, there are companies such as Sprint, for example, that are paying upward of 8 percent on their debt. Of course, Sprint has the right to pay off its bonds, but it's in Sprint's best interest to hold on to cash because the company needs capital for further investment. If a company such as Sprint, with a solid revenue base and a large asset book (although in some financial trouble), were to issue bonds, they would trade at junk valuations. A start-up with no credit, on the other hand, is very different from a company such as Sprint in that there are plenty of avenues through which the new company can issue debt.

Because we are operating under the credit standards faced by all start-up companies, I have further shielded myself from various forms of loss by no longer using equity capital to fund operations. Instead, the operating company issues debt at a fair rate not as low a rate as a company like Sprint could access, but only a smidgen above LIBOR. As a result, the operating company is required to service debt as a portion of capital expenditures before I can receive any kind of salary. This offers the entrepreneur of a small start-up an interesting way to fund operations; it also has the added benefit of being tax efficient, so the company does not need to purchase a depreciating asset or find other means by which to lessen its tax burden.

Although I could write another whole book covering what I have gleaned from the process of writing my father's book, I conclude with what may be the most important advice my father has offered: always have an exit strategy. I thought about this element long and hard when creating the structure for the gallery and negotiating my agreement with Rebecca. In the case that the gallery does well,

Rebecca has been incentivized as a future minority shareholder to buy my equity. I would place her purchases on a schedule according to a predetermined multiple of earnings or a multiple of the gallery's asset basis. There would be little overlap in terms of who has equity and who does not. In other words, the moment Rebecca becomes an equity partner, a schedule will be drawn for further equity purchases for the total business or expansion, with further debt on a second venture on the same basis as the first. In the case of expansion, a second venture or location would allow for growth, therefore lessening costs and eliminating the need for some of the initial spending on branding and marketing costs. The second gallery could even be one that entertains a different part of the art market—much how the bridge lines discussed in the chapter on Anne Klein and the diffusion lines discussed in the chapter on Donna Karan operated.

Although there are no guarantees, I feel more comfortable and confident having put these particular safety measures in place. A frequently cited statistic says that 80 percent of all small businesses fail within 10 years and half fail within 5 years.[1] These figures are hardly comforting for entrepreneurs; however, in the case the gallery does succeed, I will be able to navigate the problems success incurs. On the other hand, if we don't succeed, the downside measures enacted will protect me from a permanent loss of capital. The drivers for growth, however, are more related to my particular industry and how the art market accepts the gallery's branding, concept, services, and products.

—Adam Taki

---

[1] Some recent studies have argued that failure rates should be separated by industry and even by geographic region. The January 2011 Dun & Bradstreet US Business Trends Report separates failure rates by sector and state: www.dnbgov.com/pdf/US_Business_Trends_Jan11.pdf.

Acknowledgments

First and foremost, thank you to those who have helped make this book possible. My son traveled the globe to meet and interview many of you, and I thank you for taking the time to do so. I apologize that many of those conversations were not a part of the final draft, but those discussions provided my son with the much needed information to understand me and the relationships I have fostered both in the United States and abroad. Thanks go to the following: Marin Alsop; Gary Brown; Christopher Cheng; Ku Hyun Chung; Shambu Das; Hideoki Furukawa; Murray Grant; Masumi Hasegawa; Takamitsu Hayashi; Rebecca Heidenberg; Myung Kwan Hyun; Kazuo Iwata; Kenji Kimura; Toko and Tomoko Komuro; Kil Hyun Lee; Seo Hyun Lee; Arthur Levine; Tonsie McAden; Melanie McCafferty; Lori Messner; Toshio Mitsuoka; Frank Mori; Anna Nearburg; Kenji Ono; Sunao Onuma; Iwao Osaki; Andrew Preston; Barry Rebo; Ricky Sasaki; Jack Schroeder; Kathy Scott; Kil Seung Sohn; Hirotaka Takeuchi; Katsuo, Kazuo, Sachio, Shigeo, and Yasuo Taki; Hiroshi and Toshiaki Tashiro; Benson Tung; Leslie Wapnitsky; Dae-Yon Won; Masayuki Yagi; and Cathy Zambetti.

Special thanks go to Naoko Matsudaira, Yoshiki Endo, and Tony Bulnes for helping my son around Tokyo, Japan; to Chisako Kato in Nagoya, Japan; to Mansoo Lee in South Korea; and to Doris To in Hong Kong.

Thank you, Melinda Jones and Lori Messner, for the invaluable support offered to both Adam and me. And I will digress to thank you for helping convince me sometimes he's right and I'm wrong. And, of course, Dr. Mortimer R. Feinberg, without your insights and experiences, this book would never have become a reality.

Sadly, three great men very dear to me lost their lives while this book was still being drafted: my good friend, Meir Amit from Israel; my former colleague with whose family I still break bread, Susumu Kodaira; and my best friend, Ricky Sasaki.

Index